HEGEMONY IN A GLOBALIZED WORLD

*A Critical Discourse Analysis of the G8–
Broader Middle East and North Africa
Partnership from 2004 to 2013*

Abdulaziz S. Abumilha, PhD

Archway Publishing books may be ordered through booksellers or by contacting:

Archway Publishing
1663 Liberty Drive
Bloomington, IN 47403
www.archwaypublishing.com
1 (888) 242-5904

ISBN: 978-1-4808-6220-3 (sc)
ISBN: 978-1-4808-6221-0 (e)

Library of Congress Control Number: 2018904860

Print information available on the last page.

Archway Publishing rev. date: 05/01/2018

DEDICATION

In memory of my father, without whose support I would not have done anything in my life. He was a great man who was ahead of his time. His passing is a lifelong pain and agony; may he rest in peace!

This accomplishment is dedicated to my mother, whom I love dearly, and also to my lovely wife. I also recognize my brothers and sisters, whose support I appreciate, especially that of my brother Ali, who was there for me in health and sickness. I also appreciate the support and encouragement of my friends.

ABSTRACT

This book addresses current educational, political, and social challenges that many marginalized countries face, especially nations in the Broader Middle East and North Africa (BMENA) region. The book examines the types of hegemony and its effects by addressing political, social, and educational ramifications. It scrutinizes the political, educational, and social history of the Kingdom of Saudi Arabia and uses the kingdom as an example for the region because of its political influence on the region. The book engages in a critical analysis of globalization and the tools thereof to highlight the advantages and disadvantages of globalization to marginalized countries. It discusses the spread of the English language in marginalized communities, together with the status of the Arabic language in both lexical and mental dimensions. Critical discourse analysis (CDA) was the methodology used to analyze the G8–Broader Middle East and North Africa (G8–BMENA) Partnership through examining documents produced by two entities in their annual meetings: first, government officials, and second, representatives of civil societies. These documents are organized by the type of discourse: first, official discourse (dominant) by government representatives, and second, public discourse by civil societies. The idea is to examine the connections and disconnections between the two discourses in the proposed reform efforts by the partnership. The book analyzes documents issued from 2004 to 2013, and it reveals evidence of a hegemonic relationship between the G8 countries, BMENA countries, and civil societies. It also uncovers some possible and dangerous political changes affecting not only BMENA but also the world.

CONTENTS

CHAPTER 1

Introduction

I start my introduction with questions that I have constantly asked myself in order to give the reader insight into the ideas that shape my thinking about this book.

- Why did I need to change who I am socially and culturally to be considered a success in the eyes of my community?
- Why was the English language imposed on me when I was six years old?
- Why did I think less of myself when I wasn't able to speak English?
- Why did I enroll in the English language department for my bachelor's degree?
- Why do Arabs look up to the West with admiration and with an opposite sentiment toward ourselves?
- Why do we try to distance ourselves from our culture and values and strive to adopt Western values?
- Why do we see a connection between the West and civilization and intellect?
- Why do we trust the West and dismiss the Rest?
- Is this just my experience, or is it a global phenomenon?

- Why do the Rest continue to send students to the West, spending billions of dollars on their education, when the money could be invested elsewhere?
- Will the Rest ever be independent to decide for itself?

I do not claim to have the answers to these questions, nor do I attempt to answer them in this book. But it is astonishing to me when I see the connection made between being educated, civilized, and enlightened and having the ability to speak English fluently or having a Western credential. This connection has been made by people across the spectrum, from people with no formal education to those with the highest educational credentials. I can share two examples, from many, that I recently experienced. First, I was in Saudi Arabia on a domestic flight (in December 2014) and found myself sitting next to an older man. Both of us were wearing a *thawb* and a *ghutra* (traditional Saudi attire). I was watching something on my iPad, and then we started a conversing in Arabic about local topics. I was very excited to hear his perspective about things in our native language, especially when I had been away from home for much of the previous ten years, except for vacations to my homeland about once a year. Then suddenly he spoke to me in English, saying, "I am an educated man." I was perplexed and disturbed by his reasoning to prove himself to me that he was an educated man *in English*, even though the entire conversation had been in Arabic and was cordial in nature. My first reaction was surprise—which I am certain he noticed by my facial expression. Subsequently, I brought the conversation back to Arabic. It was ironic that he felt a need to prove his value to me by speaking English. I suppose that he believed that by doing so he was showing me, a much younger man, that his ability to speak English was evidence that he was "educated." I was crestfallen. I had wanted to hear his perspectives on local matters, but he turned the conversation back to the topic of this book. In essence, the conversation shifted from what I considered to be one of a substantive nature to a superficial one because of his sudden use of the English language.

The second example occurred at Johns Hopkins Hospital in February 2015 when I was talking to a physician who was from East India and who was trying to hide his foreign accent. He said to me: "I don't know about your background, but you seem to be highly educated when I hear you speak in English." His comment was related to specific exams I was preparing to take and whether I needed a translator or not. These two examples—with the man on the airplane and the doctor at the hospital—were hurtful to me because of the general assumption or perception that for one to be considered educated and considered an intellectual, one must have the ability to speak English. Such a viewpoint ignores an individual's personal accomplishments in a host of other venues. It appears that this common perception is not limited to any geographical location on the map, regardless of race, color, level of education, or cultural background. I see this scenario in the Middle East and in countries in East Asia, which speaks to the ingrained or imposed ways of judging and stereotyping people.

Those two experiences, and others, have impacted me in a great way. They have altered my view of the world and its peoples. Sometimes when I speak English, I even try to introduce a heavier Middle Eastern accent—just to see the reaction of native speakers and the level of respect I might receive from them, depending on the fluency of my English. It is of a great importance to me to try to understand why this perception persists and why it is reproduced in many different cultures. It also makes me wonder: Is there a way to stop this vicious circle? Therefore, I chose to include formal documents produced by global entities, such as the United Nations, the

World Bank, the International Monetary Fund, and the Teaching English Speakers of Other Languages (TESOL) Association in my research. Not only that, but also I analyzed local documents in the Middle East region and the Gulf States to try to determine to what this phenomenon is attributed. My experience with the English language and with Western education has not been purely my own choice; rather, it was the dominant discourse in my society. At the time, I looked at immersing myself into Western culture and into the English language as a *strategic choice* to gain personal benefits, such as social status and employment. When I graduated from college with an English language degree, I was told, "Now you have the key to knowledge and science," referring to knowing the English language, which in essence meant that the Arabic language would not get me anywhere. I was happy at the time and even proud of the accomplishment. But today, I think about it differently, because I think I would be more successful and competent if I had immersed myself into other fields during my undergraduate years. It is true that English has given me the ability to see and understand the world through a different lens, but I am certain that I lost part of the original me in the transaction. I think I am lost between two, or rather many, cultures—or what Martin and Nakayama (2007) describe as living on the border. By that, they mean physically living on the border by traveling frequently to different countries, or psychologically living on the border, caused by the interaction between different people from different cultural backgrounds, which in turn creates bicultural or multicultural individuals like me.

I came to a realization that this is a macro-level challenge (one of a global structure), and it takes deeper local and global analysis, starting with my local society and its people and also by looking at different nations and their experiences with Western hegemonic influence, not only in the realm of education but also in the realms of the economy, society, and even our aspirations. My approach to this endeavor stemmed from my own transitional positionality, the result of my extended stay in the United States and of my visits to my homeland and to other nations in the Middle East. Furthermore, I write from a place of antinomy, contradiction, and internal conflict, and now I hope to re-envision a better future for my nation, my language, and my personal and collective identities from the United States rather than from my homeland. But the main reason for such contradiction is an evolution in my thinking and real understanding of the purpose of education and language. I was faced with two options, either to be a functionalist and reap as many benefits as I can because I am seen to be of a higher status according to current global arrangements, or to expose the superstructure of the world and its hierarchy. I chose the latter because I believed it was my moral obligation, and as a scholar-in-training, I needed to set my own expectations for future projects.

Statement of the Problem

In response to globalization, nations are faced with "reform" choices that do not necessarily respond to local needs, whether we are talking about education, economy, language, or even politics. In turn, policymakers and educators operate in a homogenizing fashion when looking at policy or reform (Broadfoot, 2001). I use the word *choices* loosely because I claim that some nations do not have the luxury to choose but rather must adhere to international agendas. With this in mind, I am afraid that globalization in this sense will generate inequalities, because it stems from the neoliberalism that dominates the world. It promotes competition, and with competition there are winners and losers. Therefore, we can see a "legitimized" stratification within a society and even between countries. That is to say, the system portrays itself as fair, but people do not begin from equal starting points, and when they compete for the same privileges, those studying at "bad" schools with limited resources and unequipped teachers will be the losers at the end of the day. Yet, the elite blame the "underachievers" (in their eyes), as opposed to looking at the structure critically. Hoogvelt (2001) considers globalization to be a new form of colonization. In other words, this covert arrangement in the world strips nation-states and societies of their natural right to create or reform their educational systems without foreign influences and without being guided or misguided by economic factors and neoliberal agenda. I believe that there is a greater power and structure that supersedes local communities that follow a prescribed approach, whether in educational and economic reforms or in improvements to mainly benefit the center and at the same time restrict the periphery regions' advancement. In other words, it maintains a hierarchical relationship between the West and the Rest. I argue that globalization has an increasing influence socially, politically, and educationally. The question becomes: How and why is this hegemonic relation maintained and preserved across the planet? I wonder if there is an uprising, a counterhegemonic movement, that may help us visualize alternative realities.

Book Outline

I planned to study three major areas that are inseparable in my literature review before addressing my research questions. My starting point was to go back in history and understand the genesis of the Saudi educational system. Not only that, but also I wished to go deeper and research the establishment of the country—its political and socioeconomic conditions, and the introduction of modern education. This book addresses the Saudi social structure and social stratification and also looks for contradictions between

the official purpose—dominant discourse—of education according to the government and what actually was happening with the
Saudi population and how it was affected by educational policies
or political structure.

I examined the influence of religion on the construction of
Saudi Arabia and its educational apparatus (Akkari, 2004; Moaddel,
2006; Saleh, 1986; Trial & Winder, 1950). I analyzed the stakeholders
of that time period and how they gravitated to their positions and
the reasons behind their collaboration. I was skeptical because of the
outcomes that I witness today on a wide range of issues, and therefore
I questioned these stakeholders' reasons for that collaboration.

It appears that there are two campaigns when it comes to education, one that advocates for secular and the other for traditional,
and I think it is imperative to know the basis for each. Furthermore,
I researched the foreign influence on the Saudi educational apparatus as well as the Saudi influence on other nations, either educationally or ideologically (Abir, 1988). It was equally important to
investigate the purpose and policy of education in Saudi Arabia as
the first step in my analysis, because it had a lot in common with
the Broader Middle East and North Africa region. What was the
mission and vision of introducing education in the modern sense?
I also needed to learn about the nature of the relationship between
education and society. I needed to explore the connections and
disconnections between the two and find out who and what had
shaped the Saudi social structure. Was it education that shaped
society, or vice versa? Or did different factors shape what we know
today as the Kingdom of Saudi Arabia?

My second interest in this research was the role of globalization
in education and society. Because of the global economy and the
promise of free markets, nations are under pressure to adhere to
the rules of the markets and the nations that control those markets.

Globalization influences, or rather threatens, several dimensions in many nations. That includes economic, social, political, and educational influences caused by liberalism, neoliberalism, and capitalist ideologies (Conway, 1995; Fitzsimons, 2000; King, 1995; Wells et al., 1998).

I explored cultural effects of globalization (Barber, 1996) and its influence on social structures, not only in peripheral areas but also in dominant countries such as the United States. I investigated the different types and aspects of globalization and its positives and negatives (Pieterse, 1994). We always hear that people have equal access to education and the benefits of a "free market" in the age of globalization; however, my research investigated this premise, which many consider to be a fallacy. With that in mind, locating the Saudi society or country on the globalization spectrum was useful for my understanding of this phenomenon, and it helped me understand similar trends in similar countries (Abo-Arrad, 2004).

The role of globalization is well-documented in curriculums, schools, and the overall facade of the educational apparatus. Some claim that globalization advocates use education as a hegemonic tool that perpetuates economic and social inequalities (Apple, 1990). I believe it is imperative to juxtapose the role of different countries in this dynamic, so I analyzed this dialectical relationship, not only on an educational level but also on social and political levels.

There seem to be different views in the periphery region about education, even though they have experienced the same overt or covert fashions of colonization and exploitation and, most importantly, mental decapitation. The region of the Middle East is in a state of stagnation, with many seeing the role of Western powers as the reason for this backwardness, yet at the same time, the Western influence is seen as the savior when it comes to better social, economic, and political conditions (Neal & Finlay, 2007). Therefore, I examined the global education view, regardless of economic classes or national GPD, because education—content, communication style, medium of instruction and even human values—has aspired to follow a Eurocentric model in countries such as Japan, Saudi Arabia, and Taiwan, among many others. In my research, I attempted to uncover this hegemonic discourse, even by researchers who are considered followers of critical theory. I hear some rhetoric highlighting the deficit theory that marginalized people exhibit in many areas such as science, business, and even human traits such as progressive values, honesty, and hard work (Neal & Finlay, 2007).

I looked for cross-cultural examples and reasons behind failed educational alternatives. With this work, I strive to offer hope for better education for generations to come, considering globalization pressure and challenges. In undertaking this work, I fully understood that it would not be an easy task. I did not know what the outcomes might be, but I planned to challenge the system and its structure. My view stemmed from a critical school of thought, and I planned to utilize those methods of analyzing the status quo.

The third part of my research dealt with language and its importance in human lives and its role in shaping identity. I was intrigued to know what views there are about language and its influence in communities. It is important to know the meaning or the concept of a national language to a nation. What does it mean, and is it "normal" to have only one language? The reason for my interest grew from my experience as a native speaker of Arabic. I believe Arabic is underutilized, even neglected. Not only that, but also it is not seen as an important language or even necessary to know for one's success.

The global spread of the English language is vital to address in my work because it is intricately connected to educational policies, success, socioeconomic status, social perception, and social stratification. I addressed the debate between two campaigns: one that advocated for more English and Western models, and the other that called for complete resistance. I hoped to analyze the situation critically and arrive at alternative views that might inform society and policymakers. I examined the language aspect in the Saudi society from a worldwide superstructure that was connected to globalization, race, and imperialism.

The fourth part of this book is about answering my research questions through analyzing an international initiative that was created in 2004, known as the G8[1]–BMENA[2] Partnership, which is dedicated to educational, economic, and social reforms in the Broader Middle East region, using CDA as my methodology to learn more about its inception, agenda, ideology, and outcomes. I wanted primarily to critically analyze this partnership to uncover power relations between some Western countries and the BMENA region and their understanding of reforms by looking at their expectations. This research helped me to establish connections between this partnership and the global structure discussed in the review by using the tools of CDA to understand the types of discourse, discourse control, and mind control and how they were present in the documents produced by the G8–BMENA. My analysis focused on forty-one documents published by the partnership via its two main sources: government representatives and representatives of civil societies, which I discuss in chapter 3.

---

[1] G8 and EU countries are France, Germany, Italy, the United Kingdom, Canada, China, Russia, and the United States

[2] BMENA region includes Arab and Arabic-speaking countries in addition to North Africa; Gulf States countries (GCC) Bahrain, Kuwait, Oman, Qatar, Saudi Arabia, and the United Arab Emirates; plus Afghanistan, Algeria, Egypt, Iran, Jordan, Lebanon, Libya, Mauritania, Morocco, Pakistan, Palestine, Sudan, Syria, Tunisia, and Yemen.

Purpose and Significance

The purpose of this study first was to understand education and its purpose in society. However, my main concern was education and modern education in developing countries or the so-called "Third World" countries. I needed to understand the working of the system and its role in shaping identities and realities. My specific focus was on Saudi Arabia and the BMENA region. Another important aspect of the study examined the role of globalization in creating norms and realities. The English language has a major role, and I intended to demystify its hidden agenda and point to the damage it does to the structure of society. I do not think it is just a language or a tool that helps nations achieve their potential. Rather, I assert that the English language destroys societies, values, and communication styles, and it influences expectations, intellectual abilities, and perceptions. Furthermore, the introduction and use of the English language in a nation in which English is not the primary spoken and written form of communication causes low self-esteem for second-language speakers and adds a layer of discrimination known as linguicism (Tsuda, 2008). Such discrimination affects not only ordinary people but also many intellectuals, and even me as the researcher, because I often find myself looking at the world from a colonizer lens. That is because we Saudi Arabian natives already have the expectation ingrained in our consciousness, and it is the only standard or model we know. Therefore, I examined this internalized colonizer's view from the psyche of a marginalized people. It is crucial to end the cycle of dependency and self-flagellation in order to end the reproduction of inequalities (Bourdieu, 1977). It is important to highlight the power of hegemony that marginalized people specifically adhere to, consciously or unconsciously (Gramsci, 2000).

The significance of my research is to contribute to the resistance and critical literature in the Saudi context and the BMENA region, which I believe is categorically lacking. I argue that these countries should decide for themselves when addressing and considering any type of reform. It is important to address the history of the Saudi education system in order for us to understand the status quo through highlighting the tactics used by local or international powers to domesticate the masses. I hope that my study contributes to the social reproduction theory by looking at it from two angles: first, social construction within a nation according to the type of education and medium of instruction (the English language), and second, the position of Saudi Arabia as a nation and its people in the world hierarchy.

Finally, when civilizations are faced with challenges (such as what I propose in this research), they tend to respond to challenges in one of two ways: Zealotism or Herodianism (Toynbee, 1948). Toynbee explained Herodianism as mimicry where nations try to find the secrets of the colonizer or the hegemon and then try to become like the colonizer. This appears in non-Western nations as they imitate Western models in education, language, communication styles, music, etc. On the other hand, Zealotism is a rigid and nostalgic structure that some nations use when under distress, in an attempt to fall back on the past. There are problems with the two reactions: first, mimicry is a pale imitation and can never become as good as the original, and second, Zealotism is a dead end (Toynbee, 1948). There has to be a third way to gain true psychological and mental emancipation, such as by investing in indigenous educational and social institutions.

Research Questions

1. How have the G8 and the Broader Middle East and North African (BMENA) Partnership affected and shaped educational and social reforms in the region since its establishment in 2004?
2. What type of discourse was deployed to perpetuate hegemonic and hierarchical relationships that sustain unequal status between the G8 and BMENA countries?
3. How do the G8 representatives control the BMENA public discourse?
4. How does such discourse control the mind and the action of the BMENA countries, and what are the social consequences of such control?

CHAPTER 2

Background

A Historical Look at Saudi Arabia: Political, Educational, and Social Structures

Saudi Arabia is the largest geographical and political entity in the Arabian Peninsula. Early on, the Ibn Saud royal family envisioned that improvements and investments in education would be a great tool for legitimizing the monarchy. Before indulging in the details of the establishment of the new kingdom, it is imperative to understand the sociocultural and political circumstances of the Arabian Peninsula and the region, because those circumstances were important in the construction of the region's education and society.

The most important factor in the region's construction was and remains the religion of Islam, which includes education (Trial & Winder, 1950; Moaddel, 2006; Akkari, 2004; Saleh, 1986). This takes us back to the 600s AD and the force of the new Islamic faith when it grew rapidly throughout the region and expanding to the world. The Ottoman Empire controlled most of the Arab region in 1517 and withdrew from the region in 1917. The four hundred years of Turkish rule of the region impacted the construction of all aspects of life. However, the Turks could not subjugate the inner Arabia. This was evident in a new movement in the Arabian Peninsula known today as Wahhabism, named after its leader, Muhammad Ibn Abd al-Wahhab. He was a native of the center of Arabia (Najd). The essence of his movement was to influence the tribes to return to the *pure* version of the faith and to again become Unitarians (Moaddel, 2006; Prokop, 2003; Trial & Winder, 1950). This movement became a spiritual and political one that created allegiance with the House of Saud, which became again the royal family ruling what today is known as Saudi Arabia. King Abdulaziz Ibn Saud was described as tactician and firm, both of which contributed to the unification of the tribes in 1932 that at one time feuded constantly with one another. In that year, King Abdulaziz proclaimed the rebirth of the Kingdom of Saudi Arabia.

Prior to the declaration of the kingdom as we know it today, Ibn Saud in 1926 created a smaller kingdom in the western region of Arabia; this area was known as the Kingdom of Hijaz. His educational ambitions started there; I will elaborate on this later in the following sections.

The kingdom was a poor and mostly desert region, but the collaboration of Ibn Saud and the so-called Wahhabi group's leader remained intact. Educational opportunities at that time were both formal and traditional, and the people generally were characterized as "cultured but illiterate" (Trial & Winder, 1950, p. 122). That is because people in that era were able to narrate their history, were able to recite the Quran from memory, and were exposed to poetry.

Modern Education

Traditionally, the ulema (religious scholars) had the greatest influence on educational activities. For example, the ulema opposed the collaboration with the Arabian-American Oil Co. (Aramco)

(Rugh, 1973), which was established in the early twentieth century to drill for oil. At the time, Aramco established vocational schools for the natives to equip them with the necessary knowledge and skills to work for the company. The hope was that any cultural invasion among the Saudi youth by Western values and education styles would be limited (Trial & Winder, 1950). The first sign of modern education in Arabia in the Western sense was in 1926 when Ibn Saud created the Directorate of Education by hiring an Egyptian adviser (Abir, 1988). This decision set the tone for the educational policy in Arabia for many years afterward. The Directorate of Education opened the first secondary school and reformed existing schools. The directorate also introduced modern subjects, in addition to religion and the Arabic language (traditional education) and became dominant.

From 1926 to 1931, many teachers from Egypt were hired, and some local students were sent to Egypt for education purposes. This created tension with the ulema. However, the king found it important for his new and expanding kingdom and therefore tried to pursue his agenda without confronting the religious clerics. The king also realized the value of compromise, a strategy that sometimes let him remain on the clerics' good side. During the 1930s, education was negatively impacted because of an economic recession; this gave the ulema a de facto dominance over education. For a snapshot of education status in the early twentieth century, it must be noted that the illiteracy rate was as high as 95 percent (Abir, 1988).

Modern Education 1946–1958

The Saudi government increasingly understood the importance of education and hired more teachers from Egypt and other Arabic-speaking countries, hoping to create a pool of

Saudi-educated graduates who could replace the foreign experts. However, financial difficulties hindered the acceleration of this process in the 1940s. Nevertheless, in 1946, and with the commercial exploitation of oil, the Saudi government had progressively "Egyptianized" the nation's educational system by hiring more Egyptian teachers and sending Saudi students to Egypt. Not only that, but also the government transferred the Egyptian educational model that was imposed by the United Kingdom in the era of overt colonization.

In 1949, Aramco launched its first development plan for its employees, including Saudis, by sending them to universities in the region or in the United States (Abir, 1988; Trial & Winder, 1950). Aramco was not motivated necessarily by philanthropy per se but rather by a desire to improve its operations. Abir (1988) believed that this contribution by Aramco should not be underestimated in the realm of modern education, especially in the Eastern Province of Saudi Arabia where oil is concentrated. As what could be considered as a countereffort by the ulema and probably as a compromise by the king, the ulema established their version of modern educational facilities, which focused primarily on Islamic studies and Arabic studies, including history and civilization. The ulema resented the evolution of what once was their domain (education), but they eventually realized that they could not turn back the clock. Rather, the ulema realized that they needed to be adaptive and to function in a supervisory role over education in general. It appears that this was the period when competition became visible between two educational systems: an education system controlled by religious agenda and another controlled by the state, in other words, traditional versus secular. However, the latter could not deviate from general Islamic principles or from what was perceived as Islamic at that time.

King Saud became the new king after his father's death and restored the relationships with the ulema, in part by ordering all Saudi students who were studying abroad to return home. That demand was a clear signal to the religious establishment, which was worried that foreign influence might undermine the coveted political and religious power of the ulema.

There were also other major highlights in this era, one of which was the foundation of the Ministry of Education (MOE) in 1953; that development triggered a tripling and quadrupling of the number of students and played a key role in increases in the Saudi budget allocated for education. Another highlight of the era occurred in 1957, when the first university was established in Saudi Arabia. In 1958, the MOE adopted the current three-cycle sequence of education: six years of elementary school, three of intermediate school, and three years of secondary education.

Modern Education 1959–1986

King Faisal became the new king and followed the example his father's (Abdulaziz) leadership style by keeping a strong alliance with the ulema and approaching the relationship with concessions and compromises. A historic event occurred in 1960 when female education became formalized and legal. The new king faced violent opposition from the ulema after this innovation, but Faisal established a new General Directorate of Girls' Education under the grand mufti (Abir, 1988). Consequently, education for girls fell under the control of the ulema, and this is why the kingdom has had a gender-segregated school system ever since. The segregation also included teachers. If there is a need for a male teacher to teach females, it is done via closed-circuit television. In the 1970s, female student enrollment reached 50 percent, and by the 1980s, the number of females nearly equaled the number of male students.

Ironically, in its initial stages, the ulema opposed modern education, but they controlled the educational system during Faisal's ruling period. This has affected the curriculum, as Islamic and Arabic studies constituted a third of the curriculum in all elementary school, intermediate school, and secondary school levels (Abir, 1988; Prokop, 2003). Furthermore, elementary school graduates could opt for religious studies for their remaining schooling years, but even if they did not, religion had an organic—unbreakable—relationship with Saudi state education.

In 1960, there was a slowdown in the development of the national education system due to financial constraints, and the focus shifted from increasing the number of schools to improving the quality of education (Rugh, 2002a). This period also revealed something about Saudi society and its distaste of manual work because it was not as prestigious as formal education, and that attitude led to a decrease in student enrollment in vocational and trade schools (Prokop, 2003). The greatest boom of the Saudi modern education system occurred in the 1970s and 1980s because of the increased state revenue with the expansion of the Saudi oil-production machine. The government also issued its first five-year plan for education from 1970 to 1975. It was generally characterized by massive expansion at all levels of education. Nevertheless, the quality of education suffered in both periods when foreigners were in charge of educating Saudi nationals and also when the Saudi teachers assumed powerful positions, especially at the elementary school level, because these teachers were trained by others who had low standards.

The number of students had risen in 1986 by 35 percent (Abir, 1988), and there was an impressive decline of illiteracy rates in comparison with the illiteracy rate of the 1960s. However, Abir raised a concern about the lower standards in the country. Educational programs and opportunities differed according to the geographical location and the social backgrounds of students. For example, Bedouin (nomadic) people tended to drop out of school because education did not fit their lifestyle and thus did not help them economically because they needed to work and help their families, which is not the case with middle-class Saudi society.

I believe that this marked the initial signs of divergence between social classes in Saudi Arabia. Abir (1988) stated that the Saudi statistics did not pay attention to the disparity between social classes. However, only one-third of the lower-class students make it to the intermediate level, and only 6 percent make it to the secondary level. Abir (1988) stated that middle-class and upper-class students (the urban population), especially from major towns or areas such as Hijaz and Najd, were much more prepared for modern education because they were taught by better-qualified teachers and their schools were better. Consequently, middle-class and upper-class students dominated secondary school education and also were the beneficiaries of university education abroad.

The government was aware that the first two education plans (1970–1980) focused on the schools and students in urban areas, but it planned to rectify the situation in the rural areas in its third and fourth plans (1980–1990). Interestingly, Abir (1988) claims that having minimal education in the rural areas did not hinder the ability of the "lower class" people to move up socially, and that they were accepted in the middle class.

King Fahd assumed power in 1982, and he understood the need to maintain and maybe even advance the relationship with the ulema, believing that to do so would be a great contribution to the kingdom's political stability, especially because of economic struggles, political turmoil in the region, and the struggle among the ruling class. Therefore, the ulema were the best political ally for Ibn Saud and the government. This was effective because the population could not dispute anything stemming from their "trusted" religious leaders. Consequently, the reform movement from 1960 to 1970 was reversed, and "religious" studies were again at the heart of education, at the expense of secular education (Abir, 1988).

Higher Education

According to Abir (1988), the journey of higher education in Saudi Arabia started in 1957, and there was a rivalry between the government and the ulema in establishing institutions reflecting each of their views of education. The ulema focused on religious teaching and did what was possible to attract students by giving them generous scholarships to join their institutions. The population trusted the ulema because they were seen as the true representation of their faith.

The first university, in the Western sense, was established in 1957, and it facilitated the second boom in higher education, which occurred between 1957 and 1975. The universities followed the Egyptian model, which in essence followed the British system of higher education. However, since 1975, Saudi universities have adopted the US system of higher education. In 1985, Saudi Arabia had seven universities and fourteen colleges for women, and by 2011, according to Denman and Hilal (2011), the number increased to twenty-four government universities, fifteen private universities, and twenty private colleges.

The US influence on Saudi education started with Aramco in 1958 (Abir, 1988) and was formalized in 1975 by establishing the United States and Saudi Arabia Joint Commission on Economic Cooperation, which dealt with education and was a bilateral agreement between the two countries. The ulema were not thrilled with this development, especially because of the increasing number of

Saudi students studying in the United States, which was seen as a threat to the Saudi people's faith and culture. The ulema viewed it as westernization of Saudi Arabia, and this triggered tension between the religious establishment and the government. Furthermore, conflict grew between Saudi university graduates and US university graduates because each saw the other as an economic threat to them personally and as an ideological threat to their country.

Abir (1988) acknowledged the massive development of the Saudi education system, especially when the illiteracy rate was 95 percent in the 1950s, but also questioned "whether Saudi Arabia can afford its extensive, wasteful and inadequate educational system" (p. 49).

Education in the 1990s

The status of education remained the same in the 1990s, generally balancing the relationship between modern education and the ulema and expanding education to increase the rate of students admitted to Saudi's higher education system. On the one hand, "Islam continues to be the main legitimizing source of Ibn-Saud family; however, the strong identification with Islam invites the regime's opponents to use it as a standard by which to judge their rulers" (Prokop, 2003, p. 77). Therefore, the government had to make concessions to the religious leaders and give them (even in the ideological sense) control over the educational apparatus.

In essence, the education system represented by both the state and the ulema agreed on the same message regarding education, which promoted loyalty and obedience. The state and the ulema expected education to "promote a spirit of loyalty to Islamic law by denouncing any system or theory that conflicts with it and by behaving with honesty and in conformity with Islamic tenets; it should 'awaken the spirit of Islamic struggle, fight our enemies, restore our rights, resume our glory, and fulfill the mission of Islam' and project the unity of Muslim nation" (Prokop, 2003, p. 79).

It is crucial to highlight this cooperation between the state and the ulema and its impact on Saudi society. It is clear that a political and ideological struggle existed between the two, and at the same time, it is ironic that they claimed to be working for the people without including the people in the pursuit.

Interestingly, the discipline of history taught in Saudi schools reveals an intended or perhaps casual dismissal of other histories within Saudi society. In schools, one particular region, Najd, is the focus of history books, and its people are described by Abir (1988) and Prokop (2003) as the aristocratic class. However, history books try to unify the country around the first king (and then the royal family), who unified the tribes, and show how he chose the path of Islam to do that. However, the history books neglect the bloodshed and the battles preceding the conquest of the Arabian Peninsula. Furthermore, history books also neglect to mention critical events in the neighboring countries, such as revolutions and the collaboration between the king and the United Kingdom in the early days of establishing the kingdom.

A major characteristic of the Saudi education system (Prokop, 2003; Rugh, 2002b; Roy, 1992) is its focus on rote learning, memorization, and unquestioning attitudes—because obedience is at the core of the system. Schools also lack an emphasis on analytical and creative thinking, which is not a surprise given that the system (educational and political) wants to sustain its legitimacy and domination.

Saudi Influence on Education Abroad

Prokop (2003) addressed the global Saudi influence financially and ideologically. In other words, the Saudi government was involved in spreading its interpretation of Islam through education in many parts of the world, "from Morocco to Central Asia, to Bosnia, and elsewhere in Europe ... African countries ... and [even] including a province in China" (Prokop, 2003, p. 85). This occurred either by direct funding by the government or by the Saudi missionaries around the world, including those in the United Kingdom and the United States. Furthermore, the Saudi curriculum is taught in Saudi schools in many countries that have high Saudi populations.

This was one of the reasons that the Saudi education system was attacked, especially by Western nations, because it was involved in spreading its version of Islamic teaching, which action is characterized by many as promoting extremism (Prokop, 2003; Rugh, 2002b). A great example is the 9/11 attacks on the World Trade Center in New York City in which fifteen of the nineteen hijackers were Saudi nationals. In other words, the Saudi education system found itself under more scrutiny than ever from the liberals within the country as well as from many Western nations. However, the official government response was to deny these accusations that blamed the Saudi education system. Some Saudi officials stated that education is just one way of shaping students' identities. On the other hand, the government has admitted the need for economic and educational reforms, but the debate becomes about who is proposing the reforms and the role of education in the Saudi political system. Prokop (2003) raises the following questions:

> To what extent has the education system been shaped by and used by religious, political, and socioeconomic forces and interests? What are the domestic and global factors that are undermining the current system? What are the economic and social "side-effects" of the heavy emphasis on religious teachings? What are the links—if any—between

the education system and the message propagated inside the kingdom, as well as abroad, and Islamic extremism? (p. 79)

Government's View and Policy of Education

Roy (1992) shed light on what he understands as the eight major factors in the Saudi policy of basic education, as follows:

1. The planning of education and the use of methods of instruction in a manner that is in harmony with the teachings of Islam and is derived from its principles.
2. The provision of basic religious instruction throughout the period of education, from basic through higher education.
3. Given every individual's desire for knowledge, the state must—within the limits of its resources and abilities—give the opportunity to everyone, male or female, to acquire that knowledge.
4. Within the dictates of Islam, turning to account all forms of useful human knowledge so as to develop the community and improve its way of life.
5. The methodology, writing, and teaching of science and learning, and their various forms and resources, must be in accord with an Islamic orientation.
6. The linking of education and instruction at all levels with overall national development planning.
7. The judicious use of interaction with international developments in the fields of science, culture, and literature.
8. The use of the Arabic language as the language of instruction in all subjects and at all levels, except where it is necessary for teaching to be in another language (for example, language courses) (p. 489)

The question remains whether this vision of education was reached or not. It seems that the policies are macro in nature, and that nothing is tangible. By the third plan (Roy, 1992), however, there was some evidence of being focused, at least on giving access to education to the majority of students, males and females. Yet the quality of the education was questionable. Further, education was seen as a fight against illiteracy, but that does not necessarily translate into a better economic future for the graduates. Roy asked: What then is the logic of educating them (p. 482)?

Saleh (1986) mentioned the same vision in his article, placing Islam at the core of any educational endeavor.

> The purpose of education is to have the student understand Islam in a correct comprehensive manner, to plan and spread the Islamic creed, to furnish the student with values, teaching and ideals of Islam, to equip him with the various skills and knowledge, to develop his own conduct in constructive directions to develop the society economically, socially and culturally, and to prepare the individual to become a useful member in the building of his community. (Saleh, 1986, p. 19)

He also highlighted the goals of higher education in the country, which were similar to the previously noted goals.

However, some of the desired outcomes of the development plans and the massive budgets were to decrease the number of Saudi students studying abroad and to limit the reliance on the English language as the medium of instruction in many educational institutions. Such action, I believe, functioned as a gatekeeper that prevented many students who did not have the desire to learn another language from being educated or being perceived as such. King

Abdullah started a foreign scholarship program that has sent more than 130,000 students abroad since 2006, a third of whom have studied in the United States. To give a sense of scale, the United Sates, with 15 times Saudi Arabia's population, had only 260,000 students studying abroad in 2010 (Clary & Karlin, 2011, p. 17). The purpose of the scholarship program was to qualify those students in different fields in the hope that those students would become the new reformists in Saudi Arabia when they finished their schooling. Another reason was the huge influx of new high school graduates (half of the population are younger than 24) and the limited chances of gaining access to local universities. In other words, there was no planning to contain the new graduates in the Saudi educational system.

This fact is troubling in so many ways—financially, culturally, and politically. To the observant eye, the scholarship "agreement" came after a meeting between the king and US president George W. Bush, even though we do not know the nature of the conversation between the two leaders, especially after 9/11, and the real intent of the program. The Saudi government has paid $5 billion for Saudi students' education in the United States (Kurtz, 2012). This is a red flag, because we do not know about the politics carried out behind closed doors: Was this initiative a free choice by the king, or was it demanded by Bush for other reasons, such as economic benefits to the United States or to expose Saudi youth to Western culture to promote tolerance? However, those billions of dollars could have been invested in the Saudi educational system and its universities to reduce the total dependence on Western educational models that most likely would not fit local Saudi needs and the aspirations of Saudi students.

Since the early twentieth century, when the first scholarship for Saudi students to study abroad was offered, the educational situation remains the same, with the government looking for temporary solutions to major problems rather than facing them head-on. I ask hypothetically: If the government, which is the responsible for education in Saudi Arabia, were to deal with these challenges with honesty and integrity, what would happen? I speculate that some major political changes would take place. And that belief made me wonder if these challenges are ignored purposefully to maintain the status quo. I consider this situation as the absolute opposite of Akkari's (2004) depiction of education in the second half of the twentieth century as postcolonial education, where the governments in the Middle East and North Africa (MENA) control the education apparatus for the purpose of developing nations economically and giving all individuals, regardless of their tribes, regions, faith denominations, or religious backgrounds, an equal chance for upward mobility in society.

Akkari (2004), however, stated clearly that countries in the MENA region have many similarities in their overall construction—socially, religiously, and culturally, as well as in terms of overall achievements in the realm of education, that is, increased literacy rates and access to schools. Yet, there is a common thread between them in that the system does not meet the needs of the poorest and the disadvantaged populations, and therefore those people function at the lowest rungs of their respective societies. Here, they cannot be blamed for their position in society, because we realize (Abir, 1988; Trial & Winder, 1950) that schools and teachers are better in the urban areas and that their populations are able to benefit from the financial resources and gained scholarships to get a better education than the rest of the people.

Akkari (2004) cited some reasons behind the dropout rates in MENA's region, as follows:

a.   the inadequate quantity and quality of elementary and secondary schools;

b. the excessively long distance from home to school, which is a particularly important obstacle for girls in rural areas;

c. the lack of parent responsiveness to the laws mandating compulsory schooling, in light of the low private economic returns of schooling;

d. the inability of schools to offer an attractive environment to children;

e. the economic difficulties of some families who are forced to put their children to work early. (P. 149)

Education and Society

In this section, I look into possible paradoxes in the official view of education, philosophy, and purpose and compare these with what is actually happening in Saudi society. I would like to investigate whether the education system serves all people equally. Furthermore, I seek to discover if the education system helps the political stability of the government as its main purpose, rather than providing education to the masses.

First, we will look at possible purposes and philosophies of education and try to determine if the Saudi education system aligns with any of the purposes and philosophies. This will enable us to place the education system in a certain category or give it a label. It is important to note that defining the purpose of education is difficult and depends on many factors, but nonetheless, it is imperative to navigate the possibilities. Gow (1989) states:

> The primary purpose of a liberal education … is the cultivation of the person's own intellect and imagination, for the person's own sake. … True education is meant to develop the individual human being, the person, rather than serve the state. … Formal

schooling actually commenced as an endeavor to
acquaint the rising generation with religious knowledge: with awareness of the transcendent and with
moral truths. Its purpose was not to indoctrinate a
young person in civics, but rather to teach what it
is to be a true human being, living within a moral
order. That person has primacy in liberal education. (p. 545)

Furthermore, Descartes (cited in Vaughan, 1914) believed that
the purpose of all education is "to enable one to reach sound judgment" (p. 695). Alexander (1994) indulged in extensive debate
about education and its role in advocating for peace, capitalism,
and nationalism as its purpose. However, Alexander's depiction of
the purpose of education is the following:

The purpose of education should be to define and
teach the difference between peace for oppression
and peace for liberty, the difference between com-
petitive self-interested capitalism and a laissez-faire
spirit that provides for a "harmony of interests" for
the general uplifting of society. (p. 28)

The final view I consider is the one of Rossides (1984), who depicts education and its purpose as a type of monopoly. He summa-
rizes his view of the purpose of education as such: "history's diverse
educational systems have one all-important similarity—they serve
the interests of the powerful first and foremost" (p. 16). However, he
sees the hidden purpose. Rossides claims that the purpose of education, whether agrarian or industrial, is to establish and maintain
a class difference in societies independently from any functional
purpose. Moreover, Rossides argues that the situation in modern

education becomes tricky because in a feudal society, education is openly for the elite class without hypocrisy, which is what we are witnessing today, because today people are bombarded with an elusive equality. That is to say, when lower-class students fail or drop out from modern schooling, society (the elite) blames them for their failure, neglecting the inequitable system in the first place. In other words, modern education is used to stratify society. The same idea was used in ancient Greece, medieval Europe, China, and elsewhere, which elites in these places used different marks of distinction to separate themselves from lower classes, things such as poetry and dance (Rossides, 1984). At the end of the day, the rules of modern education have evolved, but the purpose remains the same. In other words, the education apparatus functions to legitimize and protect a certain class in society that Rossides describes as *incompetent elites*, by using what seems to be an objective tool (education) that superficially claims equality and fair competition.

Saudi Social Structure

The signs of incongruence between the ruling family and the close circle of elites in Saudi Arabia and the masses started early in the newly born kingdom. Ibn-Saud had established a solid partnership with the so-called Wahhabi movement and the ulema (religious scholars) to establish the new country based on their interpretation of Islam. The message that Ibn Saud brought to the desert was received with great hopes by the nomadic tribes for whom he had brought an end to wars between them, the result of which appeared to be one entity. However, the tribal armies that were instrumental in Ibn Saud's success in establishing the kingdom were slowly but surely isolated and became antithetical to his administration and the formation of the modern country. Instead, stronger coalitions were formed between the royal family and the elite of Hijaz (western region) and the rulers of Najd (the heart of Saudi Arabia) (Abir, 1988; Moaddel, 2006). When addressing the oneness of the nation, it seems that the condition of the country and the royal family was one of inseparability.

In the late twentieth century, there was a large social divide in the country stemming from limited economic opportunities due to the country's vulnerability because of its reliance on one commodity (oil) and price fluctuations (rentier economy). This type of economy was defined by Luciani (1990) as "an economy where the creation of wealth is centered around a small fraction of the society; the rest of the society are only engaged in the distribution and utilization of this wealth" (p. 87). This situation polarized the country, one group adhering to the Islamic values (their interpretation) to awaken the nation and bring it back to the "right path," and the other group considered to be liberal reformists (Moaddel, 2006). Both groups agreed on the need for restructuring the country. However, a highlighted incident in recent Saudi history was when a group of Muslim militants took control of the Holy Mosque (Mecca) in 1979, forcing the government to consolidate with the religious movement. With that change, the government scored high on peoples' trust meters because the nation was under attack while their religion was being hijacked by extremists. Consequently, the momentum for the reformists' movement was demolished.

Saudi society in the early twentieth century (Abir, 1988; Rugh, 1973; Zuhur, 2011) is described as a society without social classes as we know it today (in the Western sense) simply because Arabia at the time consisted of mostly nomadic tribes. Exceptions were the merchants in the Hijaz region and the ulema in Najd. Changes occurred after Ibn Saud consolidated power of the new ruling class (the aristocracy). With the production of oil in 1938 and modernization efforts after World War II, the system produced new social classes and social structures. Abir (1988) claimed that this structure did not stem from wealth or education but rather from the degree of affiliation to the royal family or regional origins. However, in later stages, education was used as another crutch to stay on top of the social hierarchy, with the elites having better schools and better teachers. Furthermore, the sons of elite members of society were sent abroad to receive a better education than the rest of the people, and therefore they used educational credentials to remain at the top of the social ladder—by using what seemed to be an objective and neutral criterion.

The king's partners who helped him financially and logistically in consolidating the kingdom were incorporated into the Saudi aristocracy. It is important to concentrate on this behavior, because I believe it set the tone for the entire nation socially and made nepotism and patronage more entrenched in the society. "Together with the royal house and the ulema [these partners] are considered to be a component of the ruling class" (Abir, 1988, p. 7). Furthermore, in the 1970s, another component was added to the ruling class, which was the *umara* (chiefs of tribes). Abir depicts this situation as rule by oligarchy. The key elements in being part of the ruling class were "origin, seniority, prestige, and leadership qualities" (Abir, 1988, p. 10) in addition to the overarching element that has been aligned with Wahhabi ideology, which was the hegemonic power in the region. To further legitimize this class and its power, the ruling class established a Consultative Council and were members of it. In essence, by being followers of Wahhabism, they domesticated the population, as the movement was established on the premise of being a representation of pure Islam (Unitarian), especially with the rise of polytheism. This established the ideological power, and the Consultative Council had given them the political authority to dominate.

Moaddel's (2006) study touched on the social construction and Saudis' attitudes toward many concepts such as religion, religiosity, and democracy, among others. It is interesting to note that the lower-class people were proponents of Western-style democracy and did not see these changes as a cultural invasion. On the other hand, the elites and the upper class, keeping in mind their easier access to better education, ability to travel and study abroad, and their greater exposure to democratic ideas, were reluctant to accept democracy. This was because democracy would undermine their interests, both political and financial, and because protecting the status quo (structure) was more beneficial, especially in the rentier economy. "Rentierism thus reinforces the state's tribal origins, because it regenerates the tribal hierarchy consisting of varying layers of beneficiaries with the ruling elite on top, in an effective position of buying loyalty through their redistributive power" (Moaddel, 2006, p. 103).

In a study conducted by Khashan (1984), the author measured the perception of some Saudi university students and found that, unlike what is happening in Western universities where students strive to maintain a middle-class status, Saudi students aspired to join the wealthy segment of the society. The author attributed this to the students' family socioeconomic background, as most of the university students interviewed in his study belonged to the upper socioeconomic class. In Khashan's study, 58 percent of the students reported that they came from a high-income population, and this was reflected in their income expectations; they wanted to maintain the status quo. Interestingly, Khashan claims that "there is no clear evidence that the lower income groups are excluded from college because the regime wants to keep them out" (Khashan, 1984, p. 21). Nevertheless, he states that the bureaucracy in Saudi Arabia is corrupt, that personal relationships get things done, and that people from upper socioeconomic segments of society get better services, including education. Another argument the author makes for the greater enrollment of more affluent segments is that this segment values education more than other socioeconomic groups do. This observation, in my view, comes from anything but a critical lens, especially when considering that the author immersed himself in Saudi society. I take this stance because a reader can discern that there is a hidden message, namely that the lower-class population has deficiencies or an intrinsic dislike for education and can be also viewed as less motivated to pursue higher education or education in general. It is vital to look at the history of modern Saudi education and society to at least have a broader understanding of the social construction and stratification.

Nieuwenhuijze (1965), in his book *Social Stratification and the Middle East,* examines societies in the MENA region and how people attain a position in the middle class. He compares the situation with that of Europe, concluding that societies in general are bipolar, where one group is on the top (elite) and the other is on the bottom (the masses). His argument is about the creation of the middle class and who becomes eligible to be part of that strata. The author cautions us that we do not attribute upward mobility strictly to modern education, because elites throughout the history of humankind did not necessarily have modern education under their belts to attain their status, but rather they had different tools that sustained or prolonged their position at the top. The Saudi case is an example of this situation, where the ruling class established partnerships with representatives of the most sacred element of the masses' life (religion) to legitimize their ability to rule the nation. Also resulting from this partnership was the creation of social stratification.

Furthermore, modern education and certain credentials, for example, Western, enhanced individuals' chances to move up socially. But the question remains: Who is the major beneficiary of that, especially in the foundation of Saudi Arabia and its modern education? I believe that the answer is complicated to some. State historians and scholars would agree with the actions of the government regarding the expansion of education during the early twentieth century and its initial focus on specific regions and populations in order to stabilize the country in its initial stages. But we can look at the elite—excluding the royal family—and see whom they actually represent. We can investigate the important positions in the government and examine who occupies these positions. We realize that most, if not all, come from a common socioeconomic class, which practice not only hinders the masses' chance of moving up socially but also kills the aspiration of generations to better themselves socially, economically, and intellectually. Brichs (2013) explains it best:

> The process of creation of the Kingdom of Saudi Arabia and the consolidation of the ruling elite has led to the identification of the al-Saud family with the state, blurring distinctions between one and the other. The resource "state" is therefore under absolute control of the core elite, i.e. the royal family and their immediate circle, as are all the resources deriving from it: capital, coercion, ideology, and information. ... This distribution (monetary) took place first between the members of the royal family, then between the tribal elite comprising the founding elite of the Saudi state and finally the religious, commercial and military elites through different clientelistic mechanisms but mainly through the generation of managerial and administrative positions in the state. (p. 162)

Akkari (2004), having paid attention to the situation in the entire Middle East and North Africa region, wrote, "The least privileged and the poor are those most strongly affected by precarious situation of the education system" (p. 149). However, the Saudi education system adds insult to injury because the country is a wealthy one and has a huge amount of political and economic influence in the region and in the world. The condition of the education system does not promise a better future. That is to say, the nature of a rentier economy is not sustainable, and other economic and educational alternatives should be explored to avoid a disastrous future.

Views on Globalization

There is an interest to discover the genesis of globalization. Wallerstein (1974) suggested that it emerged in the fifteenth century under the world capitalist system. However, the term has been used on a larger scale since the 1970s (Abo-Arrad, 2004) and 1980s (Robertson, 1992). Even though globalization has been commonplace for years, Allen (2001) questions the recent tendency of Western and even global discourse about globalization and reinforcement, even though humans have been globalized for centuries. Jameson (1998) believes that a new and more intense form of globalization emerged in the late twentieth century that is different than the one in the fifteenth century. This difference was crystalized in easier movement beyond borders of commodities, ideas, and capital, among other things. This could not have happened without advanced technologies.

The discrepancy between those different globalizations was caused not only by material conditions but also by different ideas and perceptions of people who lived during these eras. Robertson (1992) believes that globalization means "the compression of the world and the intensification of consciousness of the world as a whole" (p. 8). The world has been compressed politically, economically, and by the nature of cultural relationships, not only among people but also between nation-states, which have become more interconnected. Furthermore, people perceive and discuss the world and its events differently. People see the world as smaller, and some refer to it as "a village" because of today's instant exchange of information, ideas, and even recent revolutions through media and the internet, such as the recent Egyptian revolution (Eltantawy & Wiest, 2011).

It is imperative to shed light on the nature of globalization, as Tomlinson (1999) considers it to be a multidimensional phenomenon. Previously, globalization was examined from an economic angle, but many scholars, such as Robertson (1992), have begun to investigate cultural aspects influenced by globalization. Therefore, it is pivotal to deeply understand globalization if we are to investigate it from these two dimensions. Giddens (1991) contributes to an understanding of globalization by framing it as a "dialectic of the local and the global" (p. 22). That is to say, globalization can be seen as both a homogenizing and a heterogenizing force. In essence, globalization homogenizes the world through the intensified connectedness between people, ideas, and nations, and at the same time, the world is heterogenized because people and perhaps nations become conscious of the differences between localism and globalism.

The Economic Dimension of Globalization

The economic dimension has polarized people's perception of globalization. It seems that there are two major perceptions of globalization. The first celebrates globalization, seeing it as an economic opportunity for the peripheral countries, and the second condemns globalization because of its negative consequences. Fitzsimons (2000) argues that a parallel relationship with the emergence of globalization and the neoliberalism movement exists, considering the latter as the theoretical foundation of the latest type of globalization. In other words, neoliberalism goes hand in hand with globalization. Conway (1995) describes classic liberalism in action as a civil society that consists of rational individuals who track their interests freely. King (1995) states that *liberalism* accurately describes a society only when there is a free-market exchange. Furthermore, this understanding of liberalism is tied to capitalism with the postulation that a civil society can be achieved through a capitalist economy. Wells, Carnocha, Slayton, Allen, and Vasudeva (1998) state that neoliberalism became prominent over the past two decades because of its advocacy of "free, unregulated markets coupled with aggressive individualism" (p. 324).

Globalization that aligns with neoliberalism can be seen as positive by some because it weakens formerly rigid borders between nation-states by creating a global market that, in return, eases economic activities and exchanges between different nations. Marx and Engels (1848/1985) discussed the globalizing nature of the capitalist economy, stating that "the bourgeoisie has through its exploitation of the world market given a cosmopolitan character to production and consumption in every country" (p. 83). The purpose of capitalism is to gain profit. In the same vein, Martin (2000) states that neoliberals who advocate for a capitalistic economy consider what happens in the peripheral regions by being part of globalization and that the global market is the greatest achievement since the end of world wars. In other words, neoliberalism considers nation-states as an impediment to the global market. Bryan and Farrell (1996) say it best: "The only participants who can cause real havoc in the global capital markets are the national governments themselves because they have the power to distort the market through their influence on capital flows" (p. 8). On the other hand, national governments in the "Third World" countries most likely would not disturb the current arrangement because they benefit the most from it—and the alternative might erode their elite status. With this in mind, even though nation-states in the periphery may, in theory, hinder capitalism, in actuality, capitalism needs nation-states as "a defense mechanism" (Wallerstein, 1974, 402) to protect capitalism. In other words, Wallerstein argues that the nation-state system was initiated to protect the interests of capitalists in the core as well as the interests of nation-states but at the same time he says that it hurt the nation-state system and weakened the periphery nation-states. Globally, capitalism is connected to racial constructions. Allen (2001) has argued that "the nation-state system is a type of ecosystem for the survival of the white body and white mind" (Allen, 2001, p. 480). In the global sense, I might add, the nation-state system is a type of ecosystem for the survival of the white polity as well.

This shows the complexity of the relationship between nation-states, capitalism, and neoliberalism. On the one hand, the nation-states in the core are the beneficiaries of this system for wealth accumulation via colonialism and exploitation of peripheral areas, by preventing the creation of nation-states that could resist colonization as countries. On the other hand, in order to control the capitalist economy, the nation-state system functions via strengthening borders for the nation-states, which in turn enhances nationalism in the core states.

Allen (2001) analyzed globalization through two lenses: first, through the Marxist viewpoint, which considers capitalism at the core of the global structure, and second, through critical race theory perspective, which considers that race and "white supremacy is the most totalizing" (p. 468) superstructure in globalization. Furthermore, Allen considers Marx and Engels's views that focus on *class* analysis is inadequate and instead asserts that *race* should be at the center of any globalization analysis. That is to say, the Marxist discourse fails to clearly state the role of neoliberalism in racializing the globe into white and nonwhite.

> Neoliberalism is not producing a retraction of the nation-states as much as it is restructuring of it for the further perpetuation of white identity politics in national and international domains. (Allen, 2001, p. 473)

Moreover, Allen (2001) engaged further in his critique of the Marxist view of globalization, stating that it does not acknowledge to a satisfactory degree "the European motivation, desire, and racialization for centuries of imperialism, genocide, and slavery" (p. 476).

Globalization, capitalism, and neoliberalism have shifted the function or the meaning of nation-states. To demonstrate, Harvey (1990) and Miyoshi (1993) paid attention to the economic power of the private corporations that have transitioned to be multinational and finally transnational corporations (TNCs). The TNCs, according to the maximum financial profit, moved their locations overseas, away from restrictions, seeking cheaper labor and lower taxes. This became possible because of the global market and also because of the important role of the nation-state system, controlling the economic and financial activities both in the core and periphery areas (Hirst & Thompson, 1995). Nonetheless, the intensification of the TNCs, which coincided with the *superficial* independence from colonialism after World War II, may have shifted the role of nation-states in the core, where they become unable to control the former colonies overtly and therefore used TNCs to do the job covertly (United Nations Conference on Trade and Development, 2002). As a result, it seems, these corporations are the main beneficiary of globalization.

What does globalization do? As mentioned, it means further domination over the global market by the TNCs, which results in more capital growth. On the one hand, Smith (1997) describes globalization as an "increasingly pure form of imperialism" (p. 182), and on the other, Miyoshi (1993) considers it to be "intensified colonialism" (p.750). It is perceived as such because there is acceleration in unequal development in that globalization widens the gap between the rich and poor, not only between nation-states in the core and periphery but also within nations. Therefore, we have a massive discrepancy between the top socioeconomic class and the lower ones.

The Cultural Dimension of Globalization

Globalization intends to homogenize the globe and at the same time provokes heterogenization (Barber, 1996), which shows a dialectical relationship between the two effects. In other words, people around the world consume the same products (e.g., Hollywood movies) and also adapt norms, values, and mass culture (McDonaldization) that are foreign to periphery states, where people simultaneously develop a parochial localism and nationalism by clinging to their ethnic, local, and national identities (Ritzer, 2000). Hall (1997) states that "the return to the local is often a response to globalization" (p. 33). Featherstone (1996) says, "The difficulty of handling increasing levels of cultural complexity, and the doubts and anxieties they often engender, are reasons why localism, or the desire to return home, becomes an important theme" (p. 47). Because of the huge influence of ideas, products, values, and ideologies disseminated via global avenues, people become more confused. Their local viewpoints and interpretations are no longer the only way to read and understand the world around them. Therefore, people or nations develop strong local, ethnic, and national attachments to face the homogenizing force of globalization.

The debate remains between scholars in the way they analyze globalization and determine on what they should focus on. For example, Appadurai (1996) considers globalization as more of a heterogenization story, even though he acknowledges its homogenizing force. However, Ritzer (2004) emphasizes more of the homogenization thrust of globalization, even though heterogenization is considered within the process.

Different Globalizations

The effect of globalization is not the same in different parts of the world because it is a multidimensional phenomenon: homogenization and heterogenization. Pieterse (1994) claims that globalization produces a third type of globalization called hybridization, but he cautions against missing critical aspects of globalization in different contexts, such as "the actual unevenness, asymmetry, and inequality in the global relations" (p. 54). That is to say, globalization has given people from different cultural backgrounds access to other worldviews and products, but there is uneven access for all people to offer counterviews, which thereby creates a situation where the hegemonic worldview, values, and products (the core and the transnational class) dominate peripheral areas. Therefore, the transnational classes in nation-states in periphery areas are disconnected from the population in their states, and they have more common interests with other transnational classes in other nation-states because they share economic interests, culture, and language. At the end of the day, this creates a gap between the transnational class (elite) in the periphery areas and the population of their states, because the elite adopted global economic practices and assimilated to Western cultures (Miyoshi, 1993).

This practice of the transnational class is referred to as "globalization from above." However, this triggers transnational activists to initiate globalization from below. To put it in perspective, Brecher, Costello, and Smith (2002) depict globalization from above as increasing development in communication, technologies, and transportation that at the same time causes inequality, poverty, environment and democracy destruction, and the spread of neoliberal ideology in peripheral nations. On the other hand, globalization from above gives transnational activists advanced tools to monitor human rights issues and environmental concerns by pressuring nation-states to tackle local and global concerns. This is considered globalization from below, where in essence activists use the tools provided by globalization to resist inequalities or other negatives that emanate from globalization.

Today's globalization highlights local and global problems and helps populations become aware of them via advanced communication tools. Globalization from above, which advocates for technological advancement, mass communication, the spread of the internet, and making the world smaller, is also accused of promoting colonization, domination, homogenization, inequality, exploitation, capitalism, and neoliberalism in the world. As a result, globalization triggers a resistance known as globalization from below, where activists aim to fight the negative consequences of mythological globalization. How will this resistance (globalization from below) function in the twenty-first century? Will it gain more momentum within the transnational class and periphery areas, or will it dissolve between homogenization and heterogenization?

Saudi Arabia and Globalization

Globalization is a domination of the economic, educational, and cultural aspects of life, which is considered to be colonization of the market and the mind. Abo-Arrad (2004) argues that globalization from above in the case of Saudi Arabia can be seen in the following three areas: the economy, politics, and culture. First, Abo-Arrad claims that the economic effect of globalization from above occurs when international groups engage in a capitalization process that takes over the Saudi market. Second, Abo-Arrad argues that the political effect of globalization from above is where the US influence impacts constructing nations, which creates divisions within nations. As a result, nations become unable to resist capitalism and become reliant on it to survive. Lastly, Abo-Arrad claims that the US cultural invasion is a third effect of globalization from above, whereby nations and individuals are not capable of seeking other alternatives that stem from their critical thinking and problem-solving, and instead they rely on Western models.

Abo-Arrad (2004) examined the reasons behind the entrenched globalization in Saudi Arabia and other countries in the "Third World." He argues that the strategy used to force globalization includes the freeing up of international trade, altering the flow of international investments, a technological and information revolution, and changing the role of transnational companies. However, the most important aspect of globalization is the technological advancement represented by the use of the internet and other forms of media. Abo-Arrad asserts that the main aim of globalization is cultural domination, which can be secured by other factors, such as the economy and politics.

Education as Globalizing Instrument

As an effort to explore the concept of hegemony, which I do not distinguish from globalization, Apple (1990) states that there is nothing known as a neutral educational institution. Every institution has an agenda, overt or covert, and that agenda is a result of conscious or unconscious practices. Apple sought a better understanding of the relationship between education and economic structure, and how that relationship relates to the concepts of knowledge and power. Apple wanted to find out how education plays a role in perpetuating economic inequality. Moreover, he questioned the efforts of education to preserve and distribute cultural capital.

Three aspects of education are necessary to investigate: "first, schools as institutions, second, the knowledge form, and third, the educator him or herself" (Apple, 1990, p. 3). The role of schools is creating a false consensus by teaching what is *supposedly* legitimate knowledge. Questions emerge: Who determines that knowledge to be legitimate? Whose knowledge is it? On the other hand, schools teach students a specific way to inquire, rather than letting or helping students develop their own approach to inquiry. The schools follow agreed-upon techniques that students are expected to follow (homogenization).

Intellectuals participate in creating relationships between social activity and education that make students objects of hegemony. Intellectuals legitimize the process of education and make it seem to be a fair process—yet that is an illusion. Apple (1990) suggests that reform can be attainable by educators' efforts to examine the relationship between ideology and curriculum—that is, not only by questioning how students acquire this knowledge but also by including how, and how much, collective culture is presented in schools. Furthermore, Apple questions the hidden curriculum of schools and the norms that have been taken for granted. The nature of the knowledge being taught at schools is problematic, because educators do not fully know, or they ignore, the source of the knowledge and the social strata it supports. To me, education in this scenario functions as an agent for globalization to implement its agenda.

Apple (1990) saw individuals in educational and cultural apparatuses interested in social control and reproduction of existing hierarchies. That is to say, schools are more concerned with distribution of dispositions and norms than with giving equal chances to all students to learn skills and acquire qualifications, regardless of students' societal attachments. The reason for that behavior is to maintain the hierarchical nature of societies. Apple addresses ethical obligations by researchers that make life more livable with the hope of making improvements and changes. He sees the fulfillment of that obligation as possible through collective and structured action by educators. They need to continue the journey for a more ethical and poetic understanding of curriculum in order to have a new social order and perhaps social justice.

Wexler and Whitson (1982) explored the failure and disappointing results of some radical education efforts to change the outcome of mainstream education. They noticed the active participation of students in sustaining hegemony and in the reproduction of socio-economic classes. Therefore, they believe that specific analysis of hegemony is important in order to understand the reasons behind the failure of radical changes. At first, Wexler and Whitson attempted to define hegemony as a starting point by paying attention to sociohistorical context. The authors consider hegemony as follows:

> A lived hegemony is always a process. It is not, except analytically, a system or a structure. It is a realized complex of experiences, relationships, and activities, with specific and changing pressures and limits. In practice, that is, hegemony can never be singular. (p. 31)

Moreover, hegemony is defined as "the imposition of dominant culture on non-dominant groups, particularly since the era begun by Reagan and Thatcher international economic policies" (Olaniran & Agnello, 2008, p. 69). In other words, and according to a global view, educational hegemony is imposed by economically developed countries (EDCs) on less economically developed countries (LEDCs). Olaniran and Agnello argue that the globalization era began in the 1970s by the actions of corporations and by manufacturing, in which the focus was on transferring capital, and consequently resulted in more production and sales more than anything else. Additionally, the researchers argue that the globalization movement sought not only economic reform but also educational and occupational restructuring. In essence, EDCs attempted to dictate the agenda for the world by imposing their worldview and their vision of how they wanted the world to be. In return, the less developed countries had no choice but to adhere to the rules, because "resistance is futile" (Olaniran & Agnello, 2008, p. 69). The economically developed countries have information technology, which is the tool, and capital, in the process of globalization. According to Olaniran and Agnello, globalization has divided the world into three main powers, Western Europe, the United States, and the Asian Pacific, in addition to the rest of the world, which has no choice but to form alliances with the three main powers and follow the rules.

Consequently, in order for the rest of the world to survive in the new world order, technologically underdeveloped countries must alter their educational systems and embrace the technological system. If not, it is inevitable that they will remain economically excluded and will reside at a lower economic status. Therefore, it is assumed that transforming local educational systems to become identical to the Western ones would be a successful move across the globe. Yet that would be to ignore other factors, such as the cultural, social, political, and ecological factors unique to those countries. In essence, it would be a misuse of brainpower in those nations (Olaniran & Agnello, 2008).

It is imperative to know the dimensions of education, especially in the globalization era, where societies tend to be alike in curriculum, structure, and goals because of the political nature of the world. Olaniran and Agnello (2008) state as follows:

> There is an increased realization that globalization policy implies that education control is no longer under the direct control of a given society, especially the LEDCs who have never been involved in globalization policy setting and their chances at influencing the policy is equally small at best. (p. 72) ...

> Education has long been seen as a way to control how people learn and also serves as agency for bringing about social and cultural changes and reproduction. (p. 73) ...

> The pressure is to create one global culture, education, and economy whether intentional or unintentional is a direct consequence of technology and policies perpetuated and embraced by EDCs. (p. 76)

However, there is confusion about the concept of hegemony, and that is seen in Anderson's criticism of Gramsci's work (as cited in Wexler & Whitson, 1982). Anderson wrote, "Gramsci's work [is] unsuccessful and contradictory" (p. 31). Hegemony, according to Gramsci, is more intellectual and moral leadership rather than coercive action. In addition to the former understanding of hegemony as "false consciousness," the notion of process and ideology is included to become the way a dominant social group articulates the interests of other social groups to benefit itself. This is through making the situation neutral. Wexler and Whitson see hegemony (I may add globalization) as one component of the capitalist arsenal, in addition to the processes of ideology and coercive power.

Hegemony in Wexler and Whitson's (1982) perspective is shaped by a wide range of cultural domains, including interaction and identity, organization, and education. Wexler and Whitson suggest that hegemony not only is maintained by culture and social structure but also is "accomplished in our day-to-day interpersonal relations" (p. 38). Hegemony contains any kind of opposition by making it just for display and expression. Therefore, the opposition is permitted as long as it does not challenge existing structures.

The Periphery Region

It is vital to offer background on my targeted education system(s), which are in the Middle East and North Africa. Although Saudi Arabia is my specific concentration, it is also important to investigate the educational situation in the region because of the similar cultural and educational experiences. Formal educational systems in some of these countries were initiated by colonial powers in their current compulsory modern education form. However, according to Akkari (2004), education was scarce for natives for two main reasons: First, the colonial powers did not want to provide education to the natives, which could contribute to the natives challenging the colonial power; and second, this restriction in education—especially European-language education—has maintained colonial administration and weakened pro-independence tendencies. It is important not only to know that but also to know the aftermath of these policies, which have created a stronger religious education that focuses primarily on opposing Western education and hegemony. The bottom line is that "the story of education has also been the story of post-colonial government control of education for purposes of nation building and economic development" (Akkari, 2004, p. 145). Therefore, I believe that those countries that have chosen to be *religion*-oriented have isolated themselves from the rest of the world and thus are suffering the consequences. In other words, this has diminished the slightest hope of a beautiful (in my imagination) organic relationship between traditional and secular education, because in my assessment, these two types of education are not and should not be antithetical.

Globalized Education

A one-size-fits-all global education is evidentially failing where, history shows, societies resist hegemonic endeavors, either subtly or militantly. Olaniran and Agnello (2008) raise questions about the notion that technology would save the LEDCs when in fact it does not, and instead deepens the dependence of those countries on industrial cultures and capital and further contributes to monoculturalism, which in return continues to marginalize the less developed countries and their cultures. Ironically, Olaniran and Agnello claim that if the less developed countries were to embrace technological globalization through global education policies, they would not be able to succeed, because the policymakers might change the rules of the game or the rules might not apply equally to all participants.

Neal and Finlay (2007) explored the effects of US hegemony on education in Arab societies. The purpose of the study, which was conducted in Lebanon, was to discover the type of hegemony that existed in the region, both as externally or internally hegemonic to Arab values. Neal and Finlay raise a question: "Does the spread of American business education involve the spread of progressive business values to unprogressive parts of the world" (p. 39)? Further, the authors stress the fact that education has a great role in social change, especially when there is gender inequality and corrupt leadership in the region in question. However, what the authors call "Arab values" may prevent such progressive ambitions. Yet, discussing "Arab cultural values" is beyond the scope of this book, as its relation to the outcomes of schooling or of the current economic or political atmosphere.

There is a claim that US hegemony in education might produce good results for the people because the American model has given students a chance to look at corruption differently, especially when students see the Arab traditional values as perpetuating corruption. Therefore, students adapt the progressive spirit from the American textbooks (Neal & Finlay, 2007). In other words, the hegemonic influence might help underdeveloped countries, such as Lebanon, to make desirable changes. To better understand the progressive values in question that are embedded in American textbooks, the authors investigated the following values: equity, tolerance, accountability, consultation, and transparency. The question becomes, are these values embedded in hegemony, or did they preexist in the society prior to the introduction of US or Western education? In other words, the authors were not clear about whether the US education style changes the values of the students to be progressive or if this hegemony reinforces preexisting human values.

Neal and Finlay (2007) confirm that American business education is externally hegemonic where worldwide educational systems adopt US institutions, practices, and systems. This is not necessarily bad, because it may result in fighting corruption, as claimed in the article. On the other hand, examining the idea that American education is "internally hegemonic" is not as clear as the external notion, for two reasons: First, it is incorrect and unsustainable to have Western ownership of progressive values, and second, the accuracy of measuring the change in Arab students' values because of exposure of American textbooks is hard to prove. However, the authors believe that American business education is internally hegemonic in two fashions: First, it may reinforce *preexisting* progressive values such as tolerance and consultation, and second, it may change some traditional values antipathetic to progressive values. However, I can argue that such values (transparency, accountability, and equity) used to be the norm in Arab and Islamic societies, but something in history changed that and made them seem foreign to the region, which evidentially confirms the dynamic nature of societies wherein values change according to many factors.

Neal and Finlay (2007) do not believe that "the hegemonic dominance of American systems, standards, curricula, resources, and textbooks is meeting the educational needs of students in the majority world" (p. 66). The authors have reasons to believe that the monopolization of the US mainstream ignores local issues and circumstances. Furthermore, this might prevent meaningful learning because students cannot relate knowledge to their local communities and realities. On another note, students in the Arab world would be working in the region and the constant marginalization of their realities would not help them to be creative, and therefore local issues and realities should be the center of education.

According to Neal and Finlay (2007), there are challenges to changing the status quo. First, the "completeness" of American textbooks does not allow for inner desire or allow room for local creative discussion of local problems. In addition, busy teachers do not have the time to be creative and thus rely on materials provided by schools. Second, using the English language as a medium of instruction is troubling as well, because students cannot read as fast as native speakers of English and they end up with no time to focus on local issues. Another problem is that Arab universities lack materials in Arabic that touch on local issues, and therefore busy teachers see it as practical to use the readily available option of American textbooks. Moreover, the reliance on foreign material also introduces pedagogical problems when marginalizing local issues. Neal and Finlay sum up the education struggle in the Arab world with the following statement: "There is tripartite struggle going on between hegemony, tradition, and education" (p. 67). I argue here that the profit to international companies from textbook production supersedes local interests, and this can be done in a globalized world and capitalist societies.

A Cross-Cultural Example

I am an advocate of the improvement of educational systems, because there is always an opportunity for better educational practices. But the questions are, how we can do that and who has the right to perform this laborious task? Baker (1997) discovered this after spending lengthy time in different parts of the world, including Sri Lanka, Vietnam, Morocco, Tanzania, Cuba, Ethiopia, and aboriginal Australia. Those countries represent different cultures, religions, customs, and traditions; however, they have one common feature, which Baker classifies as resistance to Western hegemonic influences. Baker found that their ways of resisting were diverse but that restoring their cultures and values was the motive (globalization as heterogenization). Most of the nations he visited follow formal teaching approaches and understand education differently.

The idea of reforming educational systems is important, but at the same time it is complicated. The process of reformation includes three primary obstacles: first, finding the legitimate entity to undertake the process; second, ensuring that the knowledge (curriculum) is legitimate and relevant; and third, utilizing the best method of implementing change. These complex situations require complex solutions, ones that stem from specific cultural contexts. In contrast, pedagogical imperialism does not produce great results but rather worsens the relationships between the dominant groups and the dominated groups. It creates interruptions and misunderstanding because minorities do not fully conform to dominance; therefore, the time for new alternatives is overdue, and hopefully trust and good intentions will be the driving force for reformation efforts.

Possible Reasons Behind Failed Educational Alternatives

Wexler and Whitson (1982) address the reasons behind the distortion of other educational alternatives to change the nature of social and educational reproduction and globalized education. The failure is attributed to external constraints and mixed agendas. First, external constraints are the result of bureaucratic states and political accountability. These political constraints determine what is attempted in schools and also distort unwanted alternatives. Mixed agendas, on the other hand, are related to the ambiguous role of teachers and their teacher–student relationships. This ambiguity results in a number of dilemmas that could be solved only if the teacher–student interpersonal relationship were repaired. However, the authors state that there is no general solution for these dilemmas, but apparently interpersonal relationships are crucial in shaping identities to fit within hegemonic systems.

Knowledge of infrastructure (Wexler & Whitson, 1982) is the way to counterhegemonic theory and practice, as well as to understanding the mechanisms that support hegemony, especially when social methods are patterned on and amenable to change. Counterhegemony means reorganization of the different elements and the belief of the possibility of change consistent with a new vision of social order. There are different means of achieving this goal, and education is one of them.

A Vision of Reform in the Globalization Era

Educational reform in the case of Saudi Arabia to resist the negative effects of globalization and hegemony could be achieved through implementing some strategies. Abo-Arrad (2004) suggests three strategies. The first is by quantitative expansion. This entails increasing the number of teacher preparation institutions at all levels, especially at the college level and in graduate programs. Furthermore, Abo-Arrad believes that increasing the acceptance capacity in higher education is crucial, especially when half of the Saudi population is under the age of twenty-four (Clary & Karlin, 2011). Second, this quantitative expansion should be *balanced* by regions, with students across the country having equal chances to access, as opposed to only the elites. I believe this would start a debate about the difference between equality and equity.

The third strategy is a qualitative expansion that entails, first, improving teaching pedagogies to include discovery, critical thinking, dialogue, knowledge induction, and problem-solving as opposed to rote methods. Second is improving curriculum to concentrate on both *national* and international issues. Third is improving students' evaluations and test scores. Fourth is a material improvement in school conditions to provide students with the needed technologies and structure that help them achieve their goals. Fifth is raising the awareness of the nature of capitalism, which advocates for unnecessary consumerism. Sixth is investing in scientific research. Abo-Arrad (2004) highlights the shocking status of research, with the entire Arab world having invested about only 1 percent of its GDP in research and development.

Furthermore, the statistics come from an American research entity (Abo-Arrad, 2004), which draws my attention, first, to the interest of American entities to assess the research centers in the Arab world, and second, to the lack of monitoring agencies in Arab

nations for such an important issue. However, the Saudi education system focuses on hard sciences that gear students to enroll
in such fields, which in turn has marginalized the importance of
sociocultural research that would address inequalities in Saudi society (Clary & Karlin, 2011). Clary and Karlin believe that the focus
on hard science is understandable because of the challenges that
accompany the design of a social science curriculum.

Abo-Arrad (2004) introduces a new educational structure that
suggests moving from the traditional Educational Ladder model
to the Educational Tree model, the latter of which advocates for
organic relationships between different fields in education and programs. The connection is rooted in a common culture and national identity so that the challenges of globalization and Western
hegemony can be faced. Hence, Abo-Arrad challenges the current
hierarchical structure, saying it prevents reform efforts.

Possible Future Reform

First and foremost, I believe that a socioeconomic analysis is
needed in Saudi society to examine the different generations that
comprise the nation. According to Yamani (2000), Saudi society
consists of three generations: those born in the 1930s in the time
when the country was united; those born in the 1950s who experienced the wealth of the oil boom; and those born in the 1970s
and 1980s who faced economic and political instability and were
exposed to unprecedented Western influence and values through
media (cultural hegemony). Yamani's focus is on the clash between
the third generation and the other generation. It has been docu-
mented that there is a huge gap between them, especially in the
areas of social and political values and in the modern economic
infrastructure. The major concern is how to create a balance between the Saudi youth reformers' openness to Western modern

values—hybridization—and local cultural values (Pieterse, 1994). The problem is that this issue has not been addressed, and therefore the dependency on Western solutions, whether in educational, economic, or political issues, remains intact. This view, especially with members of the new generation, would result in idealizing Western societies, which in turn colonizes the minds of the coming generations (creating conformity).

Most of the research I have examined is written by Western researchers, which is clear evidence of the bad situation and which makes me question the Saudi scholars and their research efforts to provide insights for policymakers about reform. What did those educators, politicians, and other researchers who were funded by the Saudi government to study in the West since the 1950s and 1960s do to reform their nation's education system? I ask this because reform can be interpreted differently according to the background of the researcher. For example, Rugh (2002a) saw a sign of education reform when there was "*increasing use of English as medium of instruction in the* [Saudi] *classroom* [emphasis added]" (p. 44). I believe it is ironic to impose another language on all students to acquire a minimum of technological development while they suffer an enormous loss of their culture, identity, and native language. In the same vein, I am not opposing everything Western. I would rather choose the necessary approach in transmitting knowledge from any possible source to make the necessary reform—and then transition to independence. We do not need to impose the English language, for example, on *all*, but only on those who need to make contact with other educational systems to facilitate the reform movement. Interestingly, Rugh (2002b) is content with the new trends in Saudi society and education because there is an increase of Western-style learning, as if critical-thinking and problem-solving approaches are Western trademarks as opposed to human traits, and also because schools increased the dose of English language and focused more on scientific subjects. It is implied that Arabic language and culture are antithetical to success and reform. In other words, Saudis need to give up their language and culture and become more *civilized* and successful—and this happens when they imitate anything Western.

A lengthy study by (Maroun, Samman, Moujaes, & Abouchakra, 2008) addresses the status quo of the educational systems and socioeconomic status of the Gulf Cooperation Council (GCC) countries, of which Saudi Arabia is one. Expenditures on public education, when viewed as a share of the Saudi GDP, from the 1980s to 2005, were almost 7 percent greater than those of many developed countries (or compared with). But ironically, these expenditures did not contribute to a desired outcome on many levels. First, the Saudi illiteracy rate remained high at 24 percent, compared with Singapore, which had an illiteracy rate of 7 percent, and Argentina, 3 percent. Second, the average enrollment rate in the GCC countries for tertiary education was 24 percent, compared with Canada, 57 percent, and the Republic of Korea, 89 percent. Third, the official Saudi unemployment rate was 15 percent (a conservative figure) in 2005. However, Bremmer (2004) claimed that the actual unemployment rate was greater than 20 percent.

Allam (2011) affirms that the Saudi government spent $38 billion of its 2011 budget on education, but again, the outcome was disappointing because of a radical resistance that had an extreme view of education. Because Saudi students ranked almost at the bottom on international assessments in science and math, a partnership has been established between the Ministry of Education and international companies to create a new curriculum to develop an education industry that will create smart schools.

One may question the future of the Saudi reform in education and in general when looking at the large number of students studying abroad and asking whether those students are functioning as agents (consciously or unconsciously) to implement the agenda of globalization or if they are working to tackle the issues in a critical way by using what they have learned to improve the nation in all areas without absolute dependency on foreign models. In other words, there has to be a breaking point in social institutions that generates solutions from within the country, and Saudi Arabia must reduce its imports and its consumption.

I consider some recommendations from different studies that address reforming the Saudi education system. Allam (2011) addresses different areas in reform, including improving curriculum so that it focuses more on math and science and less on religious studies, however, I truly believe that teaching religion and science should not conflict. Decentralization of the education system represented by the Ministry of Education, even in the private schools, is essential for future reform. Decentralization does not necessarily mean privatization.

Maroun, Samman, Moujaes, and Abouchakra (2008) believe that a holistic view of education reform is the right action for Saudi Arabia. First, the capacity of educational institutions to provide access to many students who do not have access to university-level education must be expanded. Second, education that concentrates on the market demand for highly skilled employees must be provided. The authors believe that the effect of globalization cannot be neglected but rather should be integrated into the system, with an emphasis on local values and culture. But how can this be done, especially when the Ministry of Education hires an international company to develop a national curriculum?

Third, technological development and its applications must be a focus of any educational reform. Most importantly, Maroun, Samman, Moujaes, and Abouchakra (2008) argue that the Saudi government has crafted a great strategic plan, but there is a problem with its implementation. The authors recommend involving all possible stakeholders in the educational reform process.

Critical Vision for the Future

First, we need to acknowledge that Saudi society and the reform process are complicated because of internal and external factors. There are global and international pressures because of Saudi Arabia's status in the world as an oil producer (one-third of worldwide oil production). As for educational pressure, there is an increasing demand for expanding English programs that entail cultural aspects, but limited resources have been made available to achieve this goal (Donn & Al Mathri, 2010).

Second, there is a gender inequality in the Gulf States. That is to say, 48 percent of students in high schools are females, and only 20 percent of the labor market is female. These figures call attention to the need to conduct socioeconomic studies that address the issues of gender, regional, and political inequalities.

Donn and Al Mathri (2010) introduce the idea of "soft governance," which uses noncoercive language and discursive mechanisms as tools of globalization to achieve compliance of developing countries to accept the dominance of developed countries (magistracy). Soft governance has two key features. One is in the language use, which includes "targets, outcomes, relevance of education, and education as a driver of economic prosperity" (p. 151). The second is in the labor market and includes "teacher training, public-private partnership" (p. 151).

Soft governance relies on soft tools of networking, conferences, seminars, consultations, advisory groups, and publications. The language of policy documents and publications is an important indicator of the manner in which soft governance operates in the

Arab Gulf States (Donn & Al Mathri, 2010, p. 152). In other words, the dominant development discourse comes from the lens of "world vision," or rather Western vision, which is not necessarily compatible with all regions in the world and which may trigger resistance (heterogenization). In other words, this kind of resistance may help achieve the initial goal of globalization set up by the core nations to keep the periphery regions at a lower status.

Philip Altbach (2006) states: "In a world divided into center and peripheries, the centers grow stronger and more dominant and the peripheries become increasingly marginalized" (p. 24). In essence, this makes the Gulf States race to meet the globalization requirements in higher education, and that generates problems. Donn and Al Mathri (2010) argue that privatization of higher education in the region should not diminish the creation of indigenous knowledge. The authors note that the Gulf States have become nations of consumption, not of production.

It has been proven that the Gulf States are influenced by magistracy, which could result in disastrous higher education outcomes because of current attempts to transfer Western models to the region. Ritzer (2006) calls it McDonaldization of higher education because we find the same courses and qualifications wherever we go. This analogy compares the quality control of fast food to the quality control of curriculum and courses, which are the same in private or public universities. This raises a question about the benefits of imported knowledge and its long-term benefits to the Gulf States socially, academically, and economically. In other words, educational institutions become degree-delivery machines, with no exchange of knowledge or ideas between the center and the peripheries.

Therefore, some nations recognize the need for the creation of indigenous programs based on relevant knowledge. It is imperative to ask: "Where, in the countries of the Arab Gulf States, lie capacity building, knowledge creation, and the culture of imaginative ideas that rest at the root of any civilization" (Clary & Karlin, 2011, p. 159)?

Finally, opportunities in the periphery nations do not match those in the center. The periphery nations become consumers of the created knowledge. However, the nature of knowledge is dynamic in that today's knowledge becomes dated tomorrow, and further knowledge is created. There is a need for a strategic plan for education reform, but the nature of such a plan is a key issue for development. Most of the research suggests imported plans from Western nations, but Donn and Al Mathri (2010) fundamentally disagree with this premise. The authors aspire for a reform that comes from within. Their critical view envisions creating a nation that generates knowledge, not only consumes it. Donn and Al Mathri state:

> It may be that this is indeed a challenge to center-periphery conceptions of knowledge-generated societies; however, as "international expertise" and "innovation consultants" appear to be the backbone of the establishment of such societies, we may find once again, the reins of the progress are tied to chariots built elsewhere. (p. 162)

In the same vein, the global structure stemming from the neoliberal ideology that racializes the world into whites and nonwhites tends to blame "Third World" nation-states (people of color) for their failures, which is seen, for example, in the policies of the International Monetary Fund (IMF) and the World Bank. Allen (2001) states in this regard:

> These prominent institutions do the bidding of the global white polity through blaming the educational conditions of these countries [i.e., those that are

financially dependent] on the lack of competition
rather than the globalization of white supremacy.
(p. 483)

Allen (2001) suggests alternatives to counter the effects of globalization and its instruments, first by inverting the nature of class and race relationship in the Marxist interpretation of globalization by making race at the heart of discussion, and second, by creating alliances between the powerful and privileged (whites) and the marginalized (people of color) around the world. I believe it is a great alliance to have. However, I would like to problematize the issue further: Isn't that also a form of dependency on the white savior who would help us solve our problems? Isn't that a psychological and emotional defeat for people of color, an admission that we cannot succeed without this help? I do not claim to have the answer.

Finally, if we examine the nation-state relations between Arab countries, for example, we realize how deep the divergence is between most of these countries for political, economic, and religious sectarian reasons. That saddles us, however, with the dreadful notion of nationalism, which drives people apart, as opposed to creating a collective entity. It makes me question the dysfunctional groupings in the region, such as the Pan-Arabism movement, the Arab League, and the Gulf Cooperation Council. Questions emerge: Does the current global structure fight these groups or support some so that they may continue their hegemonic endeavor? Do the ruling classes and the bourgeoisies in the periphery nations favor the current arrangements with the superstructure of the world? If yes, how can the masses break this ugly partnership of exploitation?

The Language Status in Saudi Arabia: Arabic, English, or Both?

It is important to explore different views and considerations of language. Language is tied with identity, nationalism, and culture, but there are two dominant views. Language is seen first as idealism and second as instrumentation (Volosinov, 1973; Williams, 1977). Idealism depicts language as a spirit that unifies a community of people who share the same language. Here, language is also seen as an artistic phenomenon. The second view depicts language as an instrument, and therefore, it can be analyzed in a systematic and scientific manner. In other words, language is separate from human motives and emotions. It is its own entity. To clarify the two positions of language, idealism places language in the creativity and psyche of individuals, and that entails linguistic changes. Language as an instrument is a rigid system, and any variation from the norm is considered distortion.

Arabic is the national and "official" language of Saudi Arabia and most of the Broader Middle East and North Africa (BMENA) countries. But English exists in other important capacities, which I will delve into later in the chapter. Here, I discuss the meaning of having a national language. Herder (1772/2002) demonstrates the position of European intellectuals in the eighteenth and nineteenth centuries, arguing that the role of a national language is a crucial entity in unifying nations. Herder claims that language is the "characteristic word of the race, bond of the family, tool of instruction, hero song of the fathers' deeds, and the voice of these fathers from their graves" (p. 153). That is to say, language is not one thing or entity but it consists of many important matters. Furthermore, "language is a natural product of the human spirit" (p. 150). In the same vein, Humboldt (1836/1988) sees language as "the outer appearance of the spirit of a people; the language is their spirit and the spirit their language" (p. 46). In essence, language represents the national character and identity. If we apply the view of idealism to this understanding of language, it means that a specific language in a nation is an expression of national distinctiveness, something that distinguishes one nation from other nations. On the other hand, Mill (1861/2001) argues that a nation does not fundamentally have only one language, but language here is used as an instrument to create a "fellow feeling" to unite people around the nation. But again, the idealistic view of language does not detach language from its cultural and social roots, and a language cannot be seen as only an instrument to unify a nation.

The Global Spread of the English Language

The current form of globalization goes hand in hand with the English language. The invasion of the English language around the world started with the colonization of many areas of the world by the British Empire. In a later stage, the heavy role of the United States, politically, culturally, and economically, intensified the spread of English as the language of the world and the language of capitalism (Mauranen, 2003). As a result, English became the language of business, technology, and "civilized" cultures. I add that the perception of being educated is tied to one's ability to speak English. Some scholars label English as a global language (Crystal, 2002), an international language (Smith, 1983), and the world language (Conrad, 1996), and also the world's lingua franca (Jameson, 1998; Mauranen, 2003). However, Kachru and Nelson (2001) state that other languages also have been global languages, such as Arabic, Spanish, and French, but the scale of the spread of the English language has far exceeded all predecessors. To show the magnitude of its global spread, Crystal claims that 25 percent of the world's population is able to communicate in English. It is important to signify the shift in the tactics regarding the language policy, as Canagarajah (2005) states: "While non-Western communities were busy working on one project (decolonization), the carpet has been pulled from under their feet by another project (globalization)" (p. 196). The first (decolonization) attempts to reject English, and the other (globalization) demands it.

Moreover, transnational corporations have played a major role in the use of English around the world (Gray, 2002), which in essence shows the links between money, power, and the political entity that almost solely benefits from the current arrangement. This is not to say English is used only for economic purposes; it also has an important cultural dimension. This takes me to the "English language conspiracy" mentioned in the work of Fishman (2006) that looks at language policy through a critical lens. The claim is that the British Council and TESOL International Association (US based) have successfully implemented a plan to teach the language around the world—overtly for educational goals, but also surreptitiously to empower the British Council's and TESOL International Association's policy and reap more economic benefits. These two agencies support the use of their textbooks and materials, which subtly fosters the expansion of Western culture, which in turn negatively affects local cultures and native languages. It is worth addressing an important point made by Fishman that some nations that demonstrate resistance against Western agendas—the author mentions two countries in particular, Cuba and Saudi Arabia—concentrate on teaching English heavily in their educational apparatus to resist "conspiratorial imperialists" and also to support their own agendas through the use of the English language. In other words, some nations claim to use the English language as an instrument to resist the Western hegemonies.

A question emerges: Does that work? I claim that the English language becomes a marker of distinction and a cultural capital that only few can master, which results in socioeconomic benefits. In other words, English has two negative effects: First, it functions as a gatekeeper, because students in a certain socioeconomic class can afford to attend good schools with good English-language teaching, and second, it negatively impacts a national language, culture, and identity. Al-Hazmi (2006) states that the number of Saudi students enrolling in anglicized scientific institutions has dropped from 32.4 percent in 1985 to 15.2 percent in 1992 and that the number of students enrolling in institutions that use Arabic as a medium of instruction has risen from 59.2 percent to 77.3 percent. In essence, these statistics show that students chose Arabized education, even though it was limited to social science and humanities, not necessarily out of desire, but rather to escape anglicized education (scientific and technological), because the English language is blocking their aspirations on account of their lack of English proficiency. This does not necessarily help them move upward socioeconomically.

Economic Factor

English-language teaching and the usage of the English language as a medium of instruction is a huge benefit for Western countries such as the United States, the United Kingdom, Australia, and Canada (Kaplan, 2001). International students go to those countries to learn English and to acquire academic degrees because those degrees have more weight and value in their home states and increase their chances in securing higher-paying jobs. To give a sense of scale to the contribution of international students to the US economy, the net economic contribution in the year 2011–2012 was $21.81 billion (NAFSA, 2012). Saudi Arabia has sent approximately 130,000 students (Clary & Karlin, 2011) abroad since 2005, which adds approximately $6 billion to the Saudi annual national budget (MOHE, 2013). The number of Saudi students in the United States alone is approximately 71,000 (NAFSA, 2013)—this since the scholarship program began in 2006. This makes the industry of higher education in the United States the fifth largest service (Economist Global Agenda, 2002) and also a great financial exploitation for many nations. It is also important to note the importance and value of the industry of English teaching, which entails writing and publishing textbooks, operating private language institutions, creating standardized exams, and many other endeavors. This clearly produces great financial profits, mainly for nations in the West (Gray, 2002).

Three Positions on the English Language

Tsuda (2008) addresses English-language hegemony and defines it as language domination through education, communication, and economy, among other things. However, this domination also causes an *English divide*. The English divide concept refers to a division created between English-language speakers and non-English-language speakers in terms of power and resources. In essence, Tsuda argues that this causes discrimination and inequalities. Furthermore, the English divide stratifies English-language speakers hierarchically because it creates an "English-language-based class system" (Tsuda, 2008, p. 51). That is to say, native speakers of English are at the top of the pyramid, followed by ESL speakers (English as a second language—people in India, for example) and then EFL speakers (English as a foreign language—people in Saudi Arabia), and finally at the bottom are the silent speakers (people who cannot speak English). A great analogy made by Tsuda compares the language class system to the race class system, where native speakers of English are the elite or the bourgeoisie, ESL speakers are the middle class, and EFL speakers are the working class for whom learning English becomes *a lifetime labor.* Finally, the silent class resides at the bottom of the status ladder, but it is important to mention that the classes below the native speakers strive to move up the ladder (Figure 1).

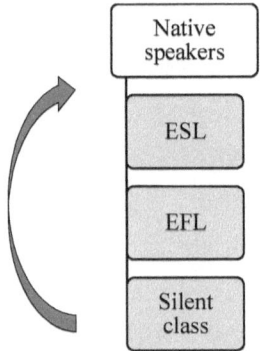

Figure 1. English-based class system

The first position regarding the spread of the English language is pro-hegemonic and is supported by many authors, such as David Crystal (a British linguist), who shows the inevitable force and domination of English around the world and claims that no other language has reached its "success" and outreach and that no one can stop its spread (Tsuda, 2008). This position has no shame in advocating for English to be the language of the world in economy, politics, education, and other venues and arenas.

The second position is called "functional/ideological" (Tsuda, 2008). It looks at English as "neutral function and functional diversity," simply to equalize the status of Standard English and nonstandard varieties of English such as Indian English or Singaporean English. As a result, the "World Englishes" term emerged and has been adopted by sociolinguists such as Braj

Kachru. Moreover, Tsuda stresses the word *ideological* in this functionalist approach because it affirms the domination of English and does not look at the power structure associated with the global spread of English.

The third position is "critical/transformative" (Tsuda, 2008). In essence, it looks at the inequality, discrimination, domination, and injustice caused by having English as the world's dominant language. It also exposes the ideological work and power structure that English maintains throughout the world. Tsuda is worth quoting at length on this matter:

> Phillipson and Pennycook are right in pointing out that we live in the world where English dominates and threatens other languages, functions as a domestic and international gatekeeper to create and reproduce the structure of inequalities between the English-speaking people and the non-English-speaking people. English hegemony causes English divide, affecting almost all the domains of our life including economy, politics, social classes, education, science, media and so on. The problems of English hegemony and English divide do not remain within the domain of language and communication, but it goes beyond that and affect all aspects of our life all around the world. (p. 49)

The Effects of English-Language Hegemony

The English language is considered a foreign language to 86 percent of the world's population (Tsuda, 2008), and to suggest that it is a language of free choice is a fallacy. This is because if nations have the free choice to use English as a medium of communication, we should ask, do they have a free choice not to adopt English? I believe the answer is no, for many reasons.

The English language not only poses a threat to the Arabic language and other native languages around the world but also imposes a Western communication style. Cameron (2002) states that the English language via globalization is "promoting particular interactional norms, genres, and speech-styles across languages, on the grounds that they are maximally 'effective' for purposes of communication" (p. 69).

This threat to native languages is described as "linguistic imperialism" by Phillipson (1992). It is perplexing that people in different nations are willing to learn the English language in order to have a better education, as Al-Jarf (2004a) reveals that 70 percent of her participants in the Saudi context prefer that English-language teaching begin at the kindergarten level. Furthermore, 50 percent of her research participants speak to their children in English at home to improve their language skills and eventually to provide them with a better education.

There is a dilemma in this situation: globalization via its "agents" demands more English-language teaching, but its spread threatens native languages, cultures, and nationalism, not only in the former colonies of the West but also in Europe. According to Eurostat (2001), 90 percent of all European students prefer to learn English at the high school level. It becomes clear through these examples that Gramsci's (2000) understanding of hegemony is evident, because his concept refers to the *willingness* of people in different countries and of different backgrounds to learn English. In other words, there is no overt coercion to adopt such educational policies, but policymakers and other people come to these conclusions through consensus. In essence, English gives people a sense of symbolic power and actual economic power. It provides them with cultural capital and projects a notion of higher status, or what Bourdieu (1977) calls *habitus*. Kachru (1984) depicts the power of the English language as "a symbol of modernization [that] offers an extra arm for success and mobility in culturally and linguistically complex and pluralistic societies" (p. 176). Therefore, people want to learn English not just because they are obsessed or mentally colonized, but also because the English language provides them with financial gains by allowing them to secure jobs.

Canagarajah's (1999) definition of pedagogical imperialism contains two characteristics. The first refers to the use of the center's textbooks and teaching materials, such as those from the United States and the United Kingdom. The second characteristic is the use of the same teaching approach that is used in the center: for example, adapting the teaching method to a process-oriented versus product-oriented approach that periphery communities such as the Tamil community in Sri Lanka use. The situation in Saudi Arabia is different. Prior to 9/11, textbooks and teaching materials were prepared by the Saudi Ministry of Education, but later textbooks began to include certain aspects of Western culture. In this case, we see a clear linguistic imperialism, but for different reasons. It is not just in the teaching of the language but also in the method of teaching and the scope.

In the same vein, Tsuda (2008) reminds us of two possible devastating outcomes of the dominance of the English language. The first is "linguicide," which means the killing of languages; this phenomenon initially was attributed to the spread of Western modernization that began in the sixteenth century. Tsuda believes that humanity has lost six thousand languages in the past five hundred years, along with the values, cultures, philosophies, and souls of the people who spoke those languages. The second outcome of English-language hegemony is "linguicism," referred to by

Phillipson (1992) as "ideologies and structures where language is the means for effecting or maintaining an unequal allocation of power and resources" (p. 55). Macedo (2003) provides an example of this outcome: some students at MIT petitioned the administration not to hire professors with foreign accents because it was difficult for them to understand their English. Here, Macedo states, "These students could have kept Albert Einstein from teaching in U.S. universities" (p. 12). This scenario demonstrates the English divide in action.

English in Saudi Arabia

Historically, and according to Al-Abed Al-Haq and Smadi (1996), English appeared in Saudi Arabia in 1924 in elementary schools, and English teaching constituted 12 percent of teaching in general. The status of the English language remained the same until 1943, when a decision was made to stop teaching English at the elementary level and instead to introduce it at the intermediate and secondary school levels. The number of classes was six per week but later was reduced to four. The debate remains the same about when to start teaching English (Al-Hazmi, 2003). English was the only foreign language taught in both regular and evening Saudi schools. In 1936, the government established the first evening school that was devoted solely to teaching English. In higher education, the first English department was established in 1957 at King Saud University for male students and in 1972 for female students. Private centers recognized the importance of English and, therefore, established the first center in 1960 for both male and female students.

Saudi Arabia falls in the third circle (expanding circle), according to the description of Kachru and Nelson (2001). This means that English is used for pragmatic purposes such as trading and communication, and for technical use. However, this status most likely will not be permanent, especially after 9/11 and its consequences on Saudi Arabia and the entire region.

The recognition of the importance of the English language was not only for educational purposes but also for Saudi ministries and public establishments, such as the Ministry of Interior, the Ministry of Defense, and the Ministry of Petroleum and Minerals. I believe this last considers English a very important asset because of the vital role of oil production in both the Saudi and global economy. The private sector was also aware of the role of English in the world and, therefore, established centers for teaching English. Also, private schools that teach English as a main subject beginning in kindergarten were established (Al-Abed Al Haq & Smadi, 1996).

The reason for introducing English in these schools was that families of high socioeconomic status wanted their children to be better educated in English than their counterparts who graduated from public schools. In addition, parents wanted their children to be exposed to Western-style education, which would help them pursue their education at Western universities (thereby lending them cultural and language capital). This approach would also help them to gain native-like competence in English.

The aims of teaching English are slightly different depending on the level in question, but at the secondary level, the aims are stated by the Ministry of Education as follows (as cited in the work of Al-Abed Al-Haq and Smadi [1996]):

- to afford the secondary school pupil a window on the world;
- to give secondary school pupils an experience of delight through reading samples of English that have universal appeal, in both arts and sciences;
- to cultivate the pupil's critical thinking, a useful adjunct to intelligent reading of English texts;

- to give play to the pupil's imagination by means of imagery in poetry and visualization of character;
- to provide the pupil who intends to join the university with an adequate knowledge of English to help him in his future studies;
- to provide the pupil who finishes his formal education with sufficient knowledge of the language to help him in his vocation; and
- to enable the pupil to gain a reasonable command of English in order to be in a better position to defend Islam against adverse criticism and to participate in dissemination of Islamic culture. (p. 461)

Al-Abed Al-Haq and Smadi (1996) surveyed fifty-four religiously committed individuals with the minimum qualification of a first university degree. The main findings of the authors were that religiously committed people in this study strongly desired the use of the Arabic language as a medium of instruction at schools and in universities for both science and humanities. However, at the same time, teaching English was seen as both a religious and nonreligious instrument. For religious purposes, English can be used in teaching non-Arab Muslims and also for preaching Islam in non-Arabic-speaking communities outside Saudi Arabia. The desire to learn English is constituted by a need for modern technological assimilation, better job opportunities, and economic development. However, I disagree with the phrase *technological assimilation*, because English prevents Saudi Arabia in the long run from being technologically independent.

The participants did not believe that teaching English would negatively influence their identities or the status of the Arabic language, citing that the two languages are used in different domains.

In other words, exposure to English does not translate to linguistic or cultural inferiority. That is because of the strong ideological and sentimental attachment to the language of one's religion. However, they believe that Arabic is more expressive, more logical, and more sacred, and thus that the religion will be sustained (Al-Abed Al Haq & Smadi, 1996). The participants differentiate between the language and its native speakers and culture, and therefore they do not correlate learning English with imperialistic purposes. That seems to be justified because of the low percentage of people in Saudi Arabia who watched or listened to foreign media at the time of the study.

New Look at the English Language in Saudi Arabia

In the wake of 9/11, Saudi Arabia was put under huge pressure from the West, especially by the United States, to enact reforms in its educational system (Elyas, 2008). The White House superficially attributed extremism to the curriculum (religious teaching) in the system. For the purpose of *Hegemony in a Globalized World*, I will focus on the demand for changes made by the United States regarding English teaching in Saudi Arabia. The United States required Saudi Arabia to begin introducing English alongside Western cultural studies in elementary schools, in an attempt to create some sort of tolerance among the Saudis toward the West and to establish understanding of the "other." However, this raises a question because the US has many subcultures: Which American culture are we talking about? This initiative faced great opposition through the media from 61 Saudi sheikhs (religious leaders), including university presidents, professors, and educators, because they thought this would lead to westernization of students and threaten local and Islamic values. Under tremendous pressure from the US government, the program was implemented, and Saudi Arabia recruited

935 English teachers from abroad. However, given the inadequate financial resources to support the program, especially after Saudi Arabia came out of the Second Gulf War, the daily number of religion classes was reduced from four to one. Teaching had become more about English and less about Islam and Arabic (Elyas, 2008). This raises a question: What kind of relationship does Saudi Arabia have with the West/United States? Regardless of the reasons behind this new policy, it says something about a hierarchical and hegemonic relationship. Elyas states:

> English is served in the Middle East, and especially in the Gulf States, as a container of ideologies which may result in reshaping the ideas impeded in it, and therefore, [it sends] the wrong messages to the society in general. ... English language was (and still is) one of the major weapons with which the West launched its massive intellectual and cultural onslaught against Muslims. (p. 36)

Therefore, the role of the English language at present has been to de-Islamize Saudi Arabia, as opposed to the situation under the British Empire. Then, the English language served as a tool for linguistic imperialism and cultural alienation. This situation in Saudi Arabia has created debate among Arab English teachers on the TESOL Islamia discussion forum. The reason is that most EFL materials in the Arab world are Euro-American inspired and do not relate to local values or issues. This role of hegemonic English could create more conflict and clash between "Us and Others" (Elyas, 2008).

Interestingly, by looking at the results of the study conducted on a group of freshmen students at King Abdulaziz University in Saudi Arabia, Al-Abed Al-Haq and Smadi (1996) found different attitudes among the students, Arab linguists, and English teachers.

The students agreed (for the most part) that teaching the English language along with Western culture is necessary to improve Saudi students' English comprehension. After the changes were made in the Saudi educational system, the students did not believe that teaching English was for imperialistic purposes or that it negatively affected their Arab identity. Half of the surveyed students believed a greater emphasis on teaching English would not negatively affect their values to the extent that their Saudi Arabian culture and Islamic identity would be diminished (Elyas, 2008). I question this notion, because the nation probably has internalized/normalized the situation. It is now abnormal when one proposes revitalization of the Arabic language, especially in today's globalized world.

Elyas (2008) suggests that because of increasing globalization, English is needed now more than ever in the Arab world and especially in Saudi Arabia, the heart of the Islamic world. After 9/11, Arabs need to know English because a lot has been said and written about them and their faith. They, more than any other peoples, need to know how to interact with the West.

The Status of Arabic and Possible Ways to Save It

Al-Jarf (2004b) advocates the importance of focusing on Arabic as a first language because of national identity, linguistic, and psychological reasons that would affect children. She believes that having a strong foundation in one's first language helps students learn a second. The author recommends correcting misconceptions that parents have about second-language acquisition by paying more attention to how schools teach English rather than when it should be taught. Interestingly, she also recommends improving the teaching of the Arabic language to make it more appealing, and she emphasizes the importance of improvements in teacher training. She suggests including attractive short stories in Arabic, which would make students interested in improving their learning and help them become more attached to their language and culture. Finally, the use of new technology, such as the internet, is important to enhance students' learning of their first language. The author's main concern is the possibility of the abandonment of the Arabic language in science, math, and other fields, caused by the domination of the English language.

Al-Jarf (2004a) conducted another study that explored the attitudes of youth toward the usage of Arabic and English as mediums of instruction. She found that 45 percent of the participants, from both the Jordanian University (Jordan) and King Saud University (Saudi Arabia), preferred to educate their children in international schools where English was the only language of instruction. On the one hand, 96 percent of the participants in the study believed that the Arabic language should be used only in the fields of Arabic literature, history, and education studies. On the other hand, the same group believed that English should be used in the fields of medicine, engineering, and computer science. Most importantly, students showed a great respect and appreciation for the English language and did not show the same for the Arabic language, and believed that because of the big gap between the two languages pertaining to terminology and research, Arabic is a crippled language.

Interestingly enough, the participants did not see Arabization efforts in the fields of medicine, engineering, pharmacy, and computers as something useful because such a process would occur only over a long period of time and would result in transliteration instead of having genuine Arabic terms. The participants saw doing so as confusing because those terminologies are attached to English more than to Arabic, and the use of the English language helps one to communicate with the rest of the world better than Arabic does. To supporting their claims, students said they did not consider the Arabic language to be a good medium of instruction at the university level because of the lack of scientific research and resources in Arabic.

Al-Jarf (2004a) stresses the important roles that should be adopted by the Arab governments to promote the use of Arabic in hospitals and companies in an attempt to limit the harm of English invasion. She also advised the Arab governments to learn from the experiences of other countries—Indonesia, Malaysia, and France—in preserving their local languages. For example, France established a French academy to protect its language by making a law that forbids the use of English words instead of French words, even if the English word is more common and widespread. On the other hand, Arabic organizations such as TESOL Arabia, unfortunately and ironically, promote the use of English as the medium of instruction in Arabic schools and universities. Al-Jarf concluded her study by warning Arabic educational institutions not to surrender to the new pressures facing their countries, especially after 9/11. She condemned the retreating status of publishing in Arabic, juxtaposed with the increasing publications in English. Misconceptions among students today who favor using English exclusively in local schooling systems need to be looked at through an ideological and a critical lens.

As an effort to promote the use of the Arabic language and to enhance its status among its speakers, Al-Zoman (2003) studied the possibilities of using Arabic letters and numbers in internet domain names instead of roman letters and numbers. Usage of the internet is an indication of a country's development, both economically and technologically. The percentage of the population in the Arab world who use the internet is 1.6, according to a 2003 report of the United Nations Development Program—and that is exceptionally low. The author believes that this could be attributed to the use of

English in the network and the possibility that not all Arabs are capable of dealing with English. Al-Zoman sees a necessity of using Arabic language instead of English on the internet to create more opportunities for a wider range of people in Saudi Arabia and the rest of the Arab world. However, this is no easy task because of the complexity of the Arabic language. For instance, the Arabic language uses diacritical marks to create different meanings and also uses a discursive writing system.

Consequently, Al-Zoman (2003) considers Arabizing internet domain names to be a vital action for future plans of electronic government and trading. Therefore, the internet should be available to all, not just to those who know English. Nevertheless, Al-Zoman strongly believes that technology should serve the language—Arabic—and not the opposite. In other words, he thinks the Arabic language should be protected from harming its core rules, such as unifying the letters instead of using each letter separately. Therefore, technology should be adjusted to serve that purpose. The solutions should be derived from the language itself and should not use solutions from other languages or incorporate characters from other languages, such as English.

Al-Jarf (2005) sheds light on the historical influence of Arabic on many languages of the world. The Arabic language holds fifth place, according to the number of speakers, which is more than 200 million speakers. On the other hand, most influential languages have borrowed heavily from Arabic. For example, English has borrowed almost 3,000 words, and Spanish more than 5,000. Al-Jarf's exploratory study showed that the situation is the reverse now. Her subjects were 350 female students at the colleges of medicine, science, pharmacy, and computer engineering at King Saud University. Her survey revealed that the English language is the medium of instruction in those colleges and that students do not study the Arabic equivalents of technical English terms because most of the textbooks are in English. The study showed that the students have misconceptions about the Arabization process. They think the process is limited to transliteration or borrowing words from other languages. As a matter of fact, students do not know about the "Saudi Arabic Terminology Databank hosted by KACST" (Al-Jarf, 2005, p. 2), an organization that deals with Arabization.

Therefore, Al-Jarf (2005) recommends the inclusion of courses in the Arabization process as part of Arabic-language requirements in those colleges. On the other hand, students at those colleges should study Arabic equivalents of English terms, and that should be part of their grades. To promote Arabization, Al-Jarf suggests that faculty members participate in this process by publishing books and articles in Arabic with Arabized terminology. In addition, Al-Jarf suggests that using Arabic should become a requirement for faculty promotions. As for the students' promoting Arabization, they should be required to write their theses or dissertations in Arabic. Finally, Al-Jarf stresses the need to familiarize students and faculty with the terminology databank and to make it accessible to them. Moreover, it is important to update the "terminology data-bank and [it] must be used in writing specialized books in Arabic" (Al-Jarf, 2005, p. 2).

The Status of Teaching English in Saudi Arabia

Al-Jarf (2004a) believes that English teachers' preparation in Saudi Arabia is problematic; therefore, on-the-job training is the way to improve their teaching through more exposure to new teaching methods. Al-Hazmi (2003) describes EFL (English as a foreign language) preparation as "nonsystematic and inadequate" (p. 341). When looking at the outcomes of teaching English at Saudi public schools, the results are not encouraging. Stimson (1980) states:

"Sadly, at the other end of the scale, six years of English teaching in the [public] schools has almost no effect at all, and many pupils can hardly utter or write a correct sentence, apart from one that has been learned by heart" (p. 1).

After studying English for eleven years in the Saudi public school system, my English-learning experience is equivalent to the findings described by Stimson (1980). This speaks to the poor teaching methods in Saudi Arabia and accounts for the time wasted on learning material not beneficial to students for future use. Therefore, I believe that the entire protocol of teaching English in Saudi Arabia should be examined and evaluated seriously. Why do officials continue to teach the language without useful teacher training, and why does the government waste resources in developing materials? I believe efforts should be directed to help promote Arabization and to retrieve the Arabic language's status in the hearts of its speakers, thus enhancing research and publications in our beloved language. It disturbs me when some participants show disrespect to the Arabic language because they think Arabic is not the language of science. Sincere efforts from the government are needed to rescue the language and to reduce independence on a foreign language or educational models, standards, and communication styles. Saudi Arabia has a wide range of problems—primarily literacy—along with educational and social issues. I believe that the right action is to focus critically on these challenges—Arabization, illiteracy, native language status, local culture—and not so much on teaching English. It is clear that not all Saudi people will learn it or have a desire to learn it. Therefore, why do policymakers focus on English? Are they interested in stratifying the society based on the possession of a language capital? Who can afford to possess it? It is apparent to me that the English language has become a marker of distinction to those at the top of the hierarchy. The claim that schools offer equal opportunities to learn English is a proven fallacy, because it takes more than six years (six hundred hours) to learn a second language and also better-equipped schools.

Reasons Behind Anglicized Higher Education in Saudi Arabia

I previously mentioned the official status of the English language set by the Ministry of Education, which is that English supposedly limited and used only when necessary to keep up with advancements in science and technology. However, in reality, English has become the official language of science and technology, and the pedagogic rationale behind using English as an instrument is described as fallacious (Troudi, 2002). Troudi delves further in his argument to pinpoint the damages inflicted on the Arabic language:

> Arabic will be seen as the language of literature, theology, social and emotional communication. Educationalists put forward many reasons as to why Arabic cannot be used to teach the sciences namely, lack of resources and textbooks in Arabic, the huge translation effort and long term projects needed for such an endeavor, and the time needed to train lecturers to switch to another language. The other argument in this competitive world, developing countries need to race against the clock to catch up with technological and industrial innovations and information technology. One needs to think of the scientists in Japan, China and Taiwan to see the weakness and fallacy of this argument. (p. 6)

Hence, this is why Al-Jarf's (2004a) participants prefer English instruction in the realm of science and prefer Arabic in other areas. That is not to say that the situation in Japan, for example, is near perfection, because English poses threats to the national language, culture, and identity (Kawai, 2004). However, I speculate that Troudi (2002) means that the Japanese language is used to a greater extent in science compared with a much worse situation for Arabic. In essence, there is a cultural and ideological division in the Saudi context and in Arab nations at large that coincides with the language division of the use of Arabic in one domain and English in another, which is described by Al-Shammary as "the most malicious conspiracies of post-colonialism" (as cited in Al-Hazmi, 2006, p. 3).

Students in higher education become victims of this language policy, in addition to further abandonment of Arabization and translation, and finally of overdependence on anglophone universities. Al-Hazmi (2006) argues that Saudi policymakers should diversify their political and educational relationships by establishing new ones with other nations, such as Japan, China, and Russia.

Future Vision for English and Arabic

An Arabization effort is one way to alleviate the status of the Arabic language among the Saudi population (Al-Hazmi, 2006; Al-Jarf, 2004a). However, Al-Abed Al-Haq (as cited in Al-Hazmi, 2003) adds that the Arabization process does not start with lexical focus but rather with psychological and ideological assessment. Al-Hazmi (2006) says in this regard: "Arabizing lexical items is of no use so long as foreign influence dominates the Arabic mentality" (p. 5).

One may ask why Arabize, because the process involves a great deal of financial and human resources? First, Al-Hazmi (2006) argues that human beings are capable of understanding thoroughly, expressing themselves clearly, and thinking creatively in their native tongue. Second, Saudi studies show positive attitudes toward using Arabic as a medium of instruction in the field of engineering, where 75 percent of faculty and 73 percent of the students in a Saudi university favor Arabic (Al-Hazmi, 2006). Furthermore, 80 percent of the surveyed medical students report that they save a third of their time when they read their materials in Arabic compared to English. Likewise, 72 percent of the students saved a third of their time when writing in Arabic compared to English, and 75 percent report that their ability to answer discussion questions is better when they use Arabic. Third, many Saudi students have a linguistic problem in the Arabic language, which has shown a clear deterioration in recent years. Al-Saad states (as cited in Al-Hazmi, 2006):

> The Ministry of Education has completely side-stepped public opinion and embarked on an extensive campaign to promote the English language at the expense of Arabic. We wished if such concern was directed at promoting Arabic at a time when the mother language is experiencing a dangerous slide at many levels. The ministry is well aware of this deterioration and possesses documents that substantiate it. The deterioration is especially evident among our college students where writing, speaking and expressing oneself in Arabic is a real problem for many. (p. 9)

Additionally, a report prepared by the United Nations (United Nations Development Program, 2003) stated that the condition of the Arabic language is severe and facing a real crisis involving vocabulary, grammar, usage, documentation, and creativity, and also in terms of theory. To show the scope of translation and

Arabization efforts in Saudi Arabia from 1931 to 1992, only 502 books were translated from foreign languages into Arabic, and all were in the social sciences (Al-Hazmi, 2006). The UNDP report found that only 4.4 books were translated from foreign languages into Arabic in the Arab world between 1980 and 1985, which means less than one book per million, juxtaposed with 519 books per million and 920 books per million in Hungary and Spain, respectively.

Arabization is not an easy task, but for it to succeed, Arab nations must move from the state of consuming knowledge to the state of producing knowledge, as stated by Donn and Al Mathri (2010), and also by Babrakzai (2002), who writes as follows:

> It is the education system of Japan, Taiwan, and Korea that are the sources of research, innovation, and production. The body of knowledge that is constantly produced and accumulated in indigenous languages, like Japanese, is then transmitted through the Japanese language in the education system. The crucial question is what knowledge, information, and technology are being produced using the Arabic language, in the Arabian Gulf countries, or in the Arab world, for that matter? (p. 43)

Al-Jarf's (2004b) work interests me because it helps me, first, to understand the nature of the teaching system in Saudi Arabia, especially during its early stages. Students need to be better motivated and have stronger engagement in their education if they wish to attain greater achievements. In short, her critique about the preaching tone in the Arabic-language classes should be reconsidered, especially when students already have many classes that teach religion. In other words, the suggestion is that Saudi Arabia should offer reading classes using Arabic for science, technology, and critical thinking.

On the other hand, according to studies of Al-Jarf (2005) and of Al-Abed Al-Haq and Smadi (1996), students' attitudes, especially in higher education, show that there is a consensus about the sole use of English as a medium of instruction. I am not in a position to make a judgment on those participants, but I inquire about the status of Arabic in the future, either in the hearts of the population or as a language of science, research, and education. I believe the way to rectify the current situation and prevent more damage to our beloved language is through Arabization efforts. Arabization efforts should be enhanced to convey knowledge from the English language and then build on a solid foundation. Arabization may appear to be a laborious task, but without empowering the language used in academia, the status of the language will continue to deteriorate.

What Can Be Done about This Dilemma?

Al-Hazmi (2006) advocates for a twofold solution to the problem of the deteriorating status of the Arabic language. First, he looked at the language policy in Saudi Arabia through a critical lens to include the Arabization process that deals with mental colonization (an ideological aspect) and the technical aspect (the lexical aspect). He and Al-Jarf (2005) acknowledge the importance of the English language, its influence, and the benefits it brings locally. However, there is a great need to improve teaching pedagogies. Al-Hazmi (2006) proposes that the "600 hours of English that students receive over a six-year period be lumped together and offered as obligatory intensive courses for science sections and optional for literary ones during the last two years of secondary school" (p. 8).

What can be done about language in education policy? Al-Hazmi (2003) and Canagarajah (2005) seem to agree on the principle that this issue should be taken to the larger local communities to determine policy. Al-Hazmi envisions the process as a bottom-up process, not top-down.

The reliance on the English language and on Western models is a symptom of a bigger problem. I think Saudi Arabia is mentally colonized, and making the matter worse is that many people consciously or unconsciously are oblivious to the issue. They choose an easier way by being functionalists to gain some benefits, instead of being morally cognizant of the role of education in a society. My hope is not to end mental colonization, because that would take decades, but I want to start a movement or organize resistance and change. I believe Palmer (2007) said it best:

> I began to see that there is a "movement mentality," in which resistance is received as a place everything begins, not ends. In this mentality, not only does change happen in spite of institutional resistance, but resistance helps change happen. The resistance itself points to the need for something new. It encourages us to imagine alternatives. And it energizes those who are called to work toward those ends. (p. 171)

Tsuda (2008) provides a counternarrative for the global spread of the English language. He outlines three possible alternatives to tackle the invasion of the English language. First, Tsuda suggests a monolingual approach, referring to choosing a politically neutral language in global communication, which may well be a language with the smallest number of speakers. The other option in this approach is using an artificial language, such as Esperanto (created by a Polish doctor in the nineteenth century). The rationale behind this approach is to debunk the English language because it is politically and culturally biased, having become the de facto language of communication without any discussion, and because it serves certain nations more than others.

The second approach offered by Tsuda (2008) is a multilingual one. That is to say, there is no need to impose one language on communication for the sake of equality between people and languages. This approach considers a language "as an important component of one's identity, pride, dignity, not just as an instrument" (p. 53). Furthermore, linguistic issues are considered a human rights issue. Therefore, Tsuda proposes the Ecology of Language Paradigm model, which perceives the linguistic issue not only as human right issue but also as environmental issue because the global ecology of language has been disturbed as we have seen in the case of linguicide.

The third approach is the Global Scheme model, which demands the creation of international law to protect languages. According to a report from UNESCO that was adopted in 2001, improvements have been made in the promotion of cultural diversity. In 2005, UNESCO adopted, by an overwhelming majority of its delegates, the Convention on the Protection and Promotion of the Diversity of Cultural Expression; only the United States and Israel opposed the agreement (Tsuda, 2008). The approach advocated for global ways of redistribution of power and resources through global taxes such as an internet tax—on internet users—to remedy the digital divide; a Tobin tax, for international speculative financial transaction; and finally, an English tax, to be levied on communication that uses the English language as the language of international communication. This fund would be allocated to the nations with less power as an effort to support affected communities. It uses the same principle of making reparations for the racial oppression and slavery mentioned in the work of Thompson-Miller and Feagin (2008) faced by African nations after colonization and also by African Americans in the United States by laws such as the Jim Crow laws.

CHAPTER 3

Methodology and Methods

I use critical discourse analysis (CDA) as my methodology. It was not an easy decision, because initially I wanted to capture every aspect and consider every angle of the issue, but a decision had to be made. However, I need to distinguish between discourse analysis (DA) and CDA. The purpose of DA is to examine the language patterns in use, depending on the researcher's approach and the understanding of language and discourse. DA has two major views related to language: the first considers language as a structure, and the second considers it to be functional. To illustrate, the structural view considers language as referential in which meanings are transmitted through the language. In other words, language is above sentence and clause level. In the functionalist perspective, language is seen as a foundation for social reality, as meanings are not transmitted but rather are created by communicators, which in part creates social reality (Shiffrin, 1994). In other words, discourse, in the functional view, is a system where social functions are realized via taking a social constructionist view, not a referential view.

It is also important to understand the researcher's point of view and approach to DA. Along these lines, DA can be categorized into four approaches (Taylor, 2001) First of these is the language itself, not the language in use, which parallels the structural view of discourse (language as referential). The remaining three approaches examine the language in use, but they are not identical because they define context differently. The second approach defines context in interpersonal situations, such as lying or arguing. The third depicts it as social and cultural, and it analyzes the language in use in situations where we have a difference in power relations, such as professor–student, doctor–patient, or superior–subordinate. And the fourth approach focuses on context in the larger society and on historical structures, such as imperialism, colonialism, inequalities, or capitalism.

Critical discourse analysis (CDA) adapts the fourth approach as its methodology, looking at discourse at the macro-level and from a historical perspective. Fairclough and Wodak (1997) recognize the following eight principles as the characteristics of CDA, which correspond with the fourth approach of discourse analysis:

1. CDA addresses social problems.
2. It considers power relations to be discursive.
3. Discourse constitutes society and culture.
4. Discourse does ideological work.
5. Discourse is historical.
6. There is a mediated link between text and society.
7. CDA is interpretive and explanatory.
8. CDA is a social action.

I think it is imperative to analyze these principles, because they make CDA unique. The second, third, fourth, and eighth principles clearly suggest that language cannot be considered referential in CDA, but rather should be considered as functional, because language in this understanding generates power, does ideological work, and causes social actions, while the referential view only reflects what is out there. Principle no. 5 is a key difference because it connects the past and the present in the understanding of discourse. To illustrate, CDA takes into account different contexts, such as historical, political, economic, cultural, and social. Finally, the first principle deals with the idea of social and cultural reproduction problems stemming from unequal power relations. In this sense, CDA focuses on power relations, domination, unequal power structures, and discrimination, among other things. In other words, it attempts to interpret the reproduction of social problems that emanate from the eight issues aforementioned.

Following are some examples of what CDA has been used to analyze. For example, Hoey (1996) analyzed the definitions of *men* and *women* in English-language dictionaries; van Dijk (1996) analyzed newspaper articles on illegal immigration in the United Kingdom; van Dijk also in (1997) analyzed the political discourse in the parliament or congress of countries such as the United States, the United Kingdom, and France; Fairclough (1995) analyzed how magazines represent women traditionally and the public discourse about the marketization of higher education; and Aronowitz (1988), Apple (1979), Bourdieu (1984), Bourdieu et al. (1994), and Giroux (1981) were all engaged deeply utilizing critical discourse analysis to demystify the purpose of education and its role in society.

CDA applies a theoretical and methodological perspective to discourse. That is to say, it is not a method or a theory that can be applied to social problems (van Dijk, 2001a). For this reason, researchers must conduct a thorough theoretical analysis of the social problem in question in order to choose which discourse and social structures are to be analyzed. Once that has been done, the researcher must come up with a suitable research method that is dependent on the characteristics of the data, on research question(s), and on the researcher's philosophical or theoretical positions. Because CDA does not offer specific procedures or pathways for analyzing discourse but rather offers a perspective or framework, the researcher must generate appropriate methods for analysis that correspond with his or her theoretical conceptualization of their study. Therefore, CDA differs from positivistic research (Taylor, 2001) in that the latter separates theories from methods in the sense that well-established methods would produce "objective" or "bias-free" knowledge. In other words, CDA integrates theories and methods (Wodak, 2001b), which theories inform methods, and those methods should not conflict with the theories.

What is the difference between DA and CDA? The latter analyzes discourse critically or is what van Dijk (2001a) called "discourse analysis with attitude" (p. 96). CDA follows epistemological and ontological assumptions that stem from Western Marxism and focuses on cultural issues that fall under the rubric of capitalism. It is argued by Fairclough and Wodak (1997) that CDA is grounded in Marxist theories by the Frankfurt school, and by the discourse perspectives of Gramsci, Althusser, Volosinov, and Foucault. The meaning of *critical* or *critique*, according to Fairclough (1995), is "to uncover or demystify the relationships of interconnected things." It is because of the fact that concepts such as hegemony, ideology, and power, on which CDA and critical studies focus, are not visible or obvious. Critical studies aim to investigate the status quo or what is called *common sense* because ideology represents itself as such and because hegemony is maintained by social consent. It is what has been naturalized in a society that might be problematic. CDA as a qualitative method of research aims to critique how meanings are made. Furthermore, CDA aims to understand and explain social norms and inequality. It also questions how power is realized in a society through language.

CDA attempts to connect the micro (discourse) with the macro (society and its structure and stratification/power), which seems not to be obvious (Fairclough, 1995; van Dijk, 1993, 2001a, 2001b; Wodak, 2001a). The question then becomes: What mediates between discourse and society? It appears that the definition of the CDA approach determines this aspect. For instance, on the one hand, for Halliday (1994), the critical linguist, Hodge and Kress (1993) consider the ideological function of grammar and linguistic aspects, such as vocabulary, grammatical structures, and word choice, to be the mediator between discourse and society. On the other hand, for van Dijk (1993), it is a shared social cognition that mediates text and power structure—and that is the position I take in this analysis.

Discourse Research and Social Structures

In this research, I focused on educational discourse, even though it was a difficult task to precisely isolate it from other discourses, such as political and economic, because these are intertwined and closely connected. The second part of van Dijk's question when using CDA as a methodology is: What is the social structure that interests me as the researcher? The social structures that interested me were those of the Broader Middle East and North African (BMENA)[3] countries and the social consequences

---

[3] BMENA region includes Arab and Arabic-speaking countries in addition to North Africa; Gulf States countries (GCC) Bahrain, Kuwait, Oman, Qatar, Saudi Arabia, and the United Arab Emirates; plus Afghanistan, Algeria, Egypt, Iran, Jordan, Lebanon, Libya, Mauritania, Morocco, Pakistan, Palestine, Sudan, Syria, Tunisia, and Yemen.

resulting from the partnership with the Group of Eight (G8)[4] countries.

The G8–BMENA Partnership was formed in 2004, and the official rationale behind its establishment was defined by the US Department of State at length as the following:

> From an idea of partnership to a growing reality, the Broader Middle East and North Africa (BMENA) Initiative represents genuine co-operation between the G8 and European nations and the governments, business and civil society of the region, in order to strengthen freedom, democracy and prosperity for all. The leaders of the G8 industrialized nations and countries of the BMENA launched the Partnership for Progress and a Common Future—a blueprint for how G8 and Middle Eastern countries could best work together to support indigenous calls for reform—at the G8 Sea Island, Georgia, summit in June 2004. Since then, a number of supportive nations and international financial institutions have offered to support and lead various initiatives elaborated at Sea Island, and the role of civil society has become increasingly significant.
>
> Governments and people of the region have expressed their wish to see democracy and freedoms expanded. The inaugural Forum for the Future in Rabat in December 2004 established a process of dialogue among G8 and regional governments in

---

[4] G8 and EU countries are France, Germany, Italy, the United Kingdom, Canada, China, Russia, and the United States.

pursuit of these aims and underwrote seven ambitious initiatives formulated at the Sea Island summit. Since the first Forum, civil society groups and lead partner countries have made significant advances in this agenda and focused on transparency of governance, women in the workplace, legal reform and human rights.

The yearly Forum for the Future is a centerpiece of the BMENA partnership by providing an international venue to support the reform voices in the region. The Forum permits the partners and other supportive countries and organizations to engage on political, economic and social reform on a regular basis. (U.S. Department of State Archives, 2001-2009)

In looking at this partnership, my approach is to understand the underlying agenda of this initiative, which includes anything related to education and educational policies and reforms produced by the governments of these countries and their representatives. The time frame I chose for my analysis is the period between the establishment of this partnership in 2004 to its final meeting in 2013. I included official documents[5] produced by the G8, by BMENA countries, and by the civil societies in their annual meetings that I was able to have access to online or that I gained access to after contacting several international organizations. The following questions guided and limited my study:

---

[5] These include any documents pertaining to education and educational policy published by G8 and BMENA countries from 2004 to 2013 from their annual meetings.

1. How has the G8 and the Broader Middle East and North African (BMENA) Partnership affected and shaped educational and social reforms in the region since its establishment in 2004?

2. What type of discourse was deployed to perpetuate hegemonic and hierarchical relationships that sustain unequal status between the G8 and BMENA countries?

3. How do the G8 representatives control the BMENA public discourse?

4. How does such discourse control the minds and the actions of people of the BMENA countries, and what are the social consequences of such control?

Conceptual and Theoretical Framework

As stated, van Dijk (2001b) proposes that critical discourse analysis (CDA) neither follows a specific research direction nor follows a unitary theoretical framework. We can have different types of critical discourse analyses because of the previously cited eight principles that guide CDA, which result in diverse theoretical and analytical approaches. That is to say, the analysis of news conferences or newspapers is different from the analysis of daily conversations, even though there is an overarching theoretical and conceptual framework. This is because of the type of questions that specifically address discourse structures and how they are deployed in the process of reproduction of dominance, and this can be in newspapers, in reports, and even in conversations. Consequently, scholars of CDA highlight vocabulary that addresses the notions of dominance, power, institutions, reproduction, and social order, among other things. With this in mind, I focus on the following four concepts to develop a critical, theoretical framework that relates or mediates discourse, cognition, and society.

Macro vs. Micro

The reason for choosing the CDA as my research methodology is that I intended to bridge the gap between the micro and macro-levels of analysis. It is this relationship between the two that forms one unit of every conversation or experience we have or observe. On one hand, microanalysis addresses language use, word choices, and verbal interaction. And on the other hand, macroanalysis focuses on dominance, power, and inequality between social groups or even between nation-states. For example, when a group such as the G8 holds an annual meeting, it is micro-level discourse and social interaction that occur between the G8 countries and BMENA representatives. But at the same time, it is macro-level in nature, because the outcome might produce a fundamental piece of policy or educational reform that might contribute to unequal status. The outcome also might contribute to the BMENA countries continuing to function in a consuming way and also might contribute to sustaining their dependence on the West and on the existing hegemonic relationship. I intend to use four aspects for my analysis to showcase how I would bridge the gap between the microanalysis and macroanalysis in my study.

- Members/groups: Members of the G8 groups (ministers of education, finance, and so forth) use discourse as representatives of group(s), institutions, or countries, and consequently, groups may act through their representatives.
- Actions/process: The action, process, or recommendation taken by individuals is an integral part of the social group or institution.
- Context/social structure: The annual meeting of Forum for the Future, led by the G8, represents a discursive interaction between all parties involved and is a foundation for a social structure seen in news conferences and in publications. In

this scenario, it is a local and global context that constricts or shapes the discourse.

- Personal/social cognition: Representatives of both the G8 and the BMENA nations have personal and social cognitions that might also be shared by the group they created. In essence, this creates a group culture and social cognition that influences the individual discourse and results in a joint action by the entire group.

Power as Control

The notion of power is an integral feature of CDA (van Dijk, 2001b), especially social power and, in my analysis, group power, the G8. We can look at power in terms of the ability to control or dominate other groups and their actions. The G8 would have more power or less power based on the degree of influence on the acts or the minds of the BMENA countries. The G8's ability to control is generated from a superior position (privilege) in light of scarce resources, such as fame, status, and money, and for my specific purpose, knowledge, experience, and access to the educational setting.

Different types of power are worth mentioning, but the type of power I am interested in is not coercive but rather is the power that is seen as "natural" or as "common sense" by the dominated groups. Power, in my understanding, is not absolute, because the dominated group may have the option to resist domination and also might see power as legitimate or, in extreme cases, necessary for success because of the deeply rooted submission to the hierarchical nature in our world. I also will look at the idea of "soft governance" that appears in many international group meetings.

Dominance is crystallized in the types of laws, policies, norms, and even expectations that at the end of the day become natural for dominated groups or countries. This is what Gramsci (1971) calls hegemony, which is not an obvious abuse of power but rather occurs when the dominated group adheres to the *wishes* of the powerful by consent. In other words, dominated countries surrender to the power of the G8 as if there are no other solutions to educational and social problems other than those imported from the West.

For the purpose of my analysis of power and discourse, first, van Dijk (2001b) suggests that the access to a specific discourse, such as those ministers of the G8 countries, as they rely on their respective nation's advancement in the realm of education and science, is a powerful resource in itself that gives "perceived" legitimacy to control and to dictate the best way to make improvements in the education field in the BMENA region. In other words, it is not coercion, but rather it is agreed upon by the BMENA countries, because the G8 countries are a clear example of success and advancement in the realm of education. Second, our actions are controlled by our minds, and if the G8 could influence the minds of BMENA representatives, then the G8 could control their actions directly or indirectly. In short, those who can control discourse eventually can control the minds and actions of the less powerful group(s).

Public Discourse

Controlling public discourse is a prevailing symbolic power source that is represented in access to knowledge and information. van Dijk (1996) categorizes the types of control as the following: first is active control, which is seen in everyday talk, such as conversations with friends, family members, or colleagues; and second is passive control, in which we do not have control over matters such as media discourse or the type of interaction between ordinary people and police officers, tax inspectors, or bosses—and that is because people are told what to believe in and what to do.

More relevant to my research interest is the social power represented in the G8 because it has more access to and control over the public discourse. Social power is the type of control we see in different fields: teachers controlling educational discourse, professors' scholarly discourse, attorneys' legal discourse, etc. In other words, the more access, control, ownership, and influence a group has over the discourse, the more power it has. It is a discursive definition of the most important aspect of social (group) power. Therefore, it is one important aspect of CDA to analyze the power dynamic in any given context.

I am able to understand the context of discourse when I consider van Dijk's (2001b) definition of *context* as "the mentally represented structure of those properties of the social situation that are relevant for the production or comprehension of discourse" (p. 356). This would include the definition of the situation at hand: actions; general settings, such as location and time; individuals involved and their cognitions or realization to include their ideologies; knowledge; goals; and opinions. In order for the powerful group (G8) to control the context, it must control one or more of these aspects. For example, it must control the place and time for meetings, the participants (countries) who should or should not attend, and the expected outcome from the interaction.

Another pivotal feature of group power is to control the structure of the discussion and the text in addition to the context. A dialectical relationship exists between text and context, and we can see that in the powerful group when it chooses a discourse genre such as when a teacher requires an answer from a student or when a judge requires an answer from a defendant.

To put it in perspective, powerful groups (speakers) have more control or less control over the context of discourse at the expense of other groups with less power, and the powerful may abuse their power. Such a scenario could be worse when that abuse is considered legitimate or natural. van Dijk (2001b) cautions that one must not consider the text or talk as the primary embodiment of power relations between different groups; rather, the context is the primary embodiment of power relations because it can shape or reinforce the type of relationship.

Mind Control

I appreciate this aspect of Gramsci's (1971) and van Dijk's (2001b) understanding of mind control. van Dijk (2001b) claims that the first major form of power is controlling the public discourse, and the second is mind control (hegemony), which reproduces dominance. Thus, people and less powerful groups acquire their beliefs, opinions, and knowledge from different sources. First is discourse that has been considered legitimate, trustworthy, and credible, such as that of experts, professors, media, scholars, or for my study, the G8 and BMENA ministers. Second, in some instances, are participants or less powerful groups who are required to attend certain events (for different reasons), such as on-the-job training programs, job instruction, and for my study, the G8 annual meetings. Third, some discourses are conducted in a closed fashion and may exclude the public or media, which prevents any alternative narrative. Fourth, participants in dominant discourses may not have a counter-discourse that may challenge the dominant discourse or information. With this in mind, CDA tools can help me analyze domination, production, and reproduction of hierarchical relationships between the G8 countries and the BMENA region.

Research in Critical Discourse

Critical discourse analysis has proven its validity in many fields of study where we see power and domination. For example, van Dijk (2001b) sheds light on how CDA can be used in studying gender inequality, which deals explicitly with discursive dominance. CDA also examines media discourse from different angles, such as through the use of linguistic tools that are apparent when we see transitivity in syntax, speech acts, lexical structure, and modality. The benefits of such research are to point out that in the media discourse, syntactic variations are used in events to deemphasize the agency, responsibility, or perspective by passively constructing specific sentences. To illustrate my point, I include an excerpt from the British House of Commons that was cited in van Dijk's work (1997):

> We do not have vast numbers of Americans entering this country on a false basis to secure permanent residency. The whole point of this legislative change is to direct it at where the problem lies people from west Africa, not from America. ... We are talking about country of origin, culture, and religion. Those factors are important, and they cause great anxiety to our constituents. (p. 49)

We notice the concept of othering in the foregoing quotation, even though it is unwisely very explicit, as if the speaker warns about "black" immigration and claims that it has to be stopped. The political elites sell this rhetoric to the public because black immigrants come to Britain on a false premise whereas "white" Americans do not, and even if the latter do, the assumption is that they will be accepted and integrated, which will maintain the whiteness of the United Kingdom. van Dijk shares many examples of more subtle statements that create divisive public sentiments, which in essence control the public discourse. There is evidence of this now in the United States when listening to US president Donald Trump.

Keeping in mind that CDA aims to investigate the relationships between power and discourse, CDA provides a complex theoretical framework to analyze power and domination and their reproduction in text and talk. However, van Dijk (2001b) claims that there are some gaps remain ambiguous in the framework, such as the interface between discourse structures and social cognition in the local and global contexts, even though they appear in notions of ideology and power. The second gap exists between the linguistically oriented studies and social studies, because social studies hardly engage in discourse analysis, and linguistic studies ignore the power abuse and inequality that are considered theories of sociology. Therefore, integrating the two approaches would help my study to arrive at a more comprehensive and satisfactory form of CDA.

Domination Shift

After reading many critical studies, whether they are under the banner of CDA or not, I noticed a shift from overt group domination to a covert professional and institutional domination (Danet, 1984; O'Barr et al., 1978; Bradac et al., 1981; Ng & Bradac, 1993; Wodak, 1984). I am interested in the latter because of its "apparent" legitimacy and neutrality, or the portrayal of such by the dominant public, media, and political discourses that work together to reproduce and perpetuate the status quo of hierarchical structures between nations. When we look at power and dominance, we find that both are associated with different social and public domains, such as law, science, education, media, or politics. These domains are controlled by elites in those "neutral" professional institutions through their discursive and active engagements in power reproduction in these domains. One may ask: Who loses in this scenario? Because it is common sense that the more advanced group in any domain would have an advantage in creating the rules, agendas, and outcomes. The problem I see with this premise is that there is a continued dependency on the dominant group by the target population, whether they are students, clients, or citizens of a certain nation or an entire region (BMENA), not to mention the fact that lasting solutions cannot be borrowed from such foreign institutions, but I believe they need to be generated from within.

Overview of Methods

"A route that leads to the goal" is the original Greek meaning of the word *method* (Kvale, 1996, p. 4). Therefore, I plan to achieve my goal of describing, analyzing, and critiquing the status quo of the G8–BMENA Partnership and the ramification of such a collaboration on educational policy and on BMENA societies. I investigated how ideologies and hierarchical structure were created and maintained in this social group through discourse. I chose this partnership because it was mainly created after the tragic trauma of 9/11 that not only befell the United States but also affected the entire world. The inception of the G8–BMENA Partnership was in 2004, led by the United States and European countries, along with some Islamic countries, under the banner of the war on terror (Rizvi, 2004). While every decent human being would agree on the premise and purpose of this cooperation, I strongly believe that the manner was not suitable for a sustainable positive outcome and, I may add, is not beneficial for the BMENA region, the BMENA people, and eventually the world.

From the many critical discourse analysis approaches that I learned about (Fairclough, 1989, 1992, 1995; Fowler, 1985; Wodak, 1996; Lee, 2000; van Dijk, 2005, 2009; Reisigl & Wodak, 2009),

I adapt van Dijk's (2009) socio-cognitive CDA as my analysis approach. My reasoning for using his approach was because of the nature of interactions, as it investigates the dynamics between cognition, discourse, and society. van Dijk (2001b) mainly focuses on stereotypes, domination, elite power abuse, reproduction or prejudice, and resistance from dominated groups. Most importantly for my study, I look at controlling discourse and its dimensions, because once a group controls the discourse, it gains access to power. van Dijk (2005) accounts for the production and comprehension of discourse when he calls it "K-device," which is shorthand for personal, interpersonal, institutional, group, national, and cultural knowledge. van Dijk (2009) suggests that we achieve social cognition via collective mental representations resulting from consensus through interaction between groups and discourse structures.

According to van Dijk (2009), individual cognition is learned by dynamic constructs (social representation), which include values, concepts, images, and norms that are shared in social groups. These social representations are activated and maintained by discourse. It is therefore pivotal for my study to analyze global and local structures relevant to education in the G8 and BMENA meetings and in subsequent local meetings available to the public. The aspects I focused on in my analysis were coherence, lexical and topic selection, implication, and policy borrowing or generation. I relied primarily on van Dijk's (1997) approach to investigate the opaque relations between power, context, ideology, and discourse by analyzing opinions, attitudes, and the socially constructed knowledge by the G8 and BMENA representatives. His approach was useful for my study because it attends to the socially constructed knowledge between different social groups with different status levels and cultural perspectives. Therefore, it is important to highlight his understanding of what constitutes a group. Something is a group when there is shared knowledge, problems, concerns, objectives, social representations, and social identity—keeping in mind that ideological power in van Dijk's opinion can take many forms, that it occurs in different situations, and that it is not limited to the dominant group.

Data Collection Process

I collected publicly available texts generated from the G8 and BMENA meetings starting from the first annual meeting in 2004. These included official reports, declarations, recommendations, civil society recommendations, statements, summaries, and any document that I found for the Forum for the Future. The annual meetings are hosted and led by a different country each year, either from the G8 or BMENA countries. I am aware that these documents discuss numerous issues, but I plan to concentrate on education, educational policies, and social ramifications. It is important for me to analyze these documents from a critical perspective by looking at the type of relationship between the members of this coalition, focusing on power, dominance, hegemony, production and reproduction of power, and overall influence in shaping BMENA educational policies that may result in social changes.

The following research questions helped me to be more focused when analyzing the documents:

1. How have the G8 and the Broader Middle East and North African (BMENA) Partnership affected and shaped educational and social reforms in the region since its establishment in 2004?
2. What type of discourse was deployed to perpetuate hegemonic and hierarchical relationships that sustain unequal status between the G8 and BMENA countries?

3. How do the G8 representatives control the BMENA public discourse?
4. How does such discourse control the minds and the actions of people in the BMENA countries, and what are the social consequences of such control?

In addition to answering these questions, I explored the role of globalization and the English language, either in communication or as a needed tool for a more successful and stable Middle East and North African region.

CHAPTER 4

Analysis

The purpose of this study was to understand the type of relationship between the Group of Eight (G8) and the Broader Middle East and North Africa (BMENA) through critically analyzing a partnership created in 2004 by the United States called the G8–BMENA Partnership. The purpose of establishing the partnership was to reform the region educationally, economically, and socially.

I used critical discourse analysis (CDA) as my methodology to analyze the publicly available documents that were published online on different governmental websites. This chapter will include descriptions of these documents. It will include my coding system and analysis criteria. Answers for the research questions will be provided in this chapter, and they will be concisely stated in the closing remarks section in chapter 5 to bring clarity to the reader regarding my overall findings and understanding.

Documents

I found forty-one documents from two major sources. First are the official documents, reports, declarations, and statements, categorized as official discourse. These official documents were produced by either the G8 governments or their representatives and also by BMENA governments or representatives. The second set of documents was produced by civil society organizations from the BMENA region. Both sets of documents were generated in their official annual meetings or preparatory meetings since the establishment of the G8–BMENA Partnership between 2004 and 2013. Those documents were publicly available online.

By collecting data from these two different sources, my intent was to achieve a greater understanding of the partnership as well as the scope of interests that each entity had regarding the promised educational, economic, and social reforms for the BMENA region.

Coding System

I developed a coding system that emanated from my background in critical research and critical discourse analysis, focusing on domination, power relations, and reproduction. I read the documents in chronological order, starting with no previous coding system because I did not want to impose a coding system that might not be present in the data in the first place. Saldana (2013) showed a process of coding as the following: the first cycle of coding can be a range from one word, to a phrase, to an entire paragraph, or to a whole page that captures the attention of the researcher. The second cycle of coding can be the same phrases, passages, or units coded previously, or even a larger portion up to that point of the analysis. In essence, these codes provided me with a critical link between the text and the meaning, whether obvious or hidden. With this in mind, I think it is a subjective process that cannot be evaded, but in order for me to check my subjectivity, I decided to use two doctoral students and ask them to read one document (Al Hayat Arabic Newspaper, 2004) and to code it using my coding system; but the difference was in their understanding of the codes and obviously their different backgrounds. Both were women pursuing PhD degrees in the Department of Language Literacy and Sociocultural Studies at the University of New Mexico. The first participant identified herself as Mexican American and the other as White American. I came up with nine major codes and three subcodes under the umbrella of "hegemony/hierarchy." (See Table 1) for more information about the codes and their meanings. I met with the two participants once and explained my rationale behind the coding system, and they were given table 1 as explanation in case they needed it while coding the document. I personally coded eighteen important statements in the given document, and after checking the document, the two participants returned a week later, the Mexican American participant coded five identical passages with the same codes, which means we agreed on the meanings some 27.7 percent of the time. This participant had limited experience with critical research and expressed some difficulty in understanding the task and the coding system, even though we have a lot in common culturally and socioeconomically. On the other hand, the white participant, who is doing research using critical research methods, coded fourteen instances identical to my coding, which is a degree of congruence of about 77.7 percent. The intent was to have two students from different social and educational backgrounds and research interests who would bring different perspectives to the research.

Table 1

Codes and Their Meanings

Code	Meaning
Hegemony/ hierarchy	The imposition of the dominant culture on subordinate groups. It is not an obvious abuse of power, but rather the dominated groups are consenting to this domination, and some consider it as the only option for advancement (ideological work, macro-level, mental colonization). I adopted Gramsci's definition of *hegemony*.
Subcodes:	
Control	Control is defined by concrete actions, e.g., providing financial assistance, which in essence would control the agenda, outcomes, etc. It also means controlling time, location, and membership in the G8–BMENA Partnership.
Power	Power shows political, economic, and educational might through advancement in such fields. For example, industrialized democracies would have the perceived legitimacy through their power to impose their views of reform on the less advanced nations in different fields, such as education.
Subgroup	Subgroup (othering): This appears when there is a conflict between groups internationally or locally. For example, when a government interacts with a civil society organization, one sees the subtle language use that shows hierarchical relationship.

Manipulation	It means when an advanced country, for example, pushes for an economic project supposedly for the benefit of a less advanced country. It is obvious that there will be some economic benefits to that country, but the major beneficiary will be the advanced country.
Ambiguity	It shows unclear statements that may contradict with the overall purpose of the partnership in this research (G8–BMENA).
Low expectations	Suggesting basic education, or vocational training, is what the region needs now, as opposed to taking the lead to reach maximum potential.
Self-Interest	When there is a real indication from a statement that the major beneficiary is the G8.
Exclusion	Excluding a country (or countries) or an organization because there is a good chance that it may block an initiative and the overall agenda of the advanced nations. It is a representation of group power.
Discrepancy	It contradicts previous statements, or if followed, it will not result in the goal of liberation from the outside control.
Lexical Issues	Words or phrases that indicate superiority or a hierarchical relationship in the analyzed text.
Positive reform	Real investment in a local community (knowledge economy, knowledge creation, as opposed to knowledge consumption, investing in local infrastructure and research).

> The opposite would be continuous dependence on Western nations and continuing to be on the receiving end.

Note: This coding system was created specifically for the purpose of analyzing the G8–BMENA documents.

Data Organization Method

I used Dedoose, a web-based research tool that can be used in qualitative and mixed-method research. It has the option of uploading my documents and organizing them according to my two descriptors, which are discourse type (official and public) and year of publication (Figure 2).

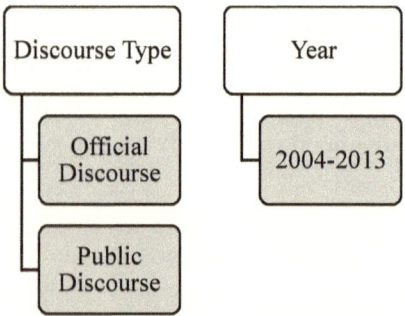

Figure 2. Descriptors used to categorize the data

Dedoose also gives the option of adding codes to text and of exporting excerpts from the data. It is a useful tool in that it provides quantitative angles to my analysis by showing the frequency and percentage of occurrences observed for each code.

Partnership Background

The purpose of this analysis is to uncover the power relation that exists between different organizations and countries and, to be more specific, to uncover the power relations in the G8–BMENA Partnership and its proposed economic, educational, and social reform for the BMENA region. I looked at the social problems that were addressed by the official entities and civil societies and there was an agreement between the two that the region has major educational, economic, and social problems, such as the following:

- A high illiteracy rate, 40 percent among the adult Arab population.
- A combined GDP of twenty-two Arab countries that is less than that of Spain.
- More than 50 million people was estimated to enter the job market by 2010.
- Only 1.6 percent of the population has access to the internet.
- Some 51 percent of adult Arabs demonstrating a desire to emigrate (United Nations Development Program, 2002)

These indicators, among others, put the region and the world on high alert, especially for security reasons. Thus, the G8–BMENA Partnership was born under the auspices of the United States and some European countries. My reasoning for choosing this partnership is because of the power relations between the West and East and the continuous hegemonic nature of this relationship, whether previously in the period of overt colonization or now because of globalization. On February 13, 2004, a draft of the partnership was leaked by an Arabic newspaper, *Al Hayat* (Al Hayat Arabic Newspaper, 2004). The surprise leak has exposed again US hegemony in the region, and it was scandalous because none of the Arab nations were involved in the drafting process of this partnership and its agenda even though it is about their own region. Sharp (2005) states:

> Arab governments, such as Egypt and Jordan, expressed frustration over *not having been part of the drafting process* [emphasis added] and expressed their dismay over having to find out about the proposal through the media rather than through consultations with the U.S. government. (p. 2)

Nevertheless, we all understand the political leverage the United States has to create the initiative and describe the status of the region and prescribe a remedy. This shows clearly the type of hegemonic and hierarchical relationship at hand, but there is more to be said about the partnership and its orchestration. One may ask: If the partnership is for the good of the region, its population, and the world, then what is the problem if the United States created it?

One of the other problems in the creation was naming the partnership, as it was called the Greater Middle East (GME), which stirred unwanted reactions, because it is such a large region that contains Arab, non-Arab, Muslim, and non-Muslim populations, and a one-size-fits-all approach would not work. Thereafter, some local governments such as Jordan and Egypt offered their concerns about the proposed reform. However, the name was changed to garner more appeal in the region without touching the essence of the previous draft to become the G8–BMENA, even though the region is even more diverse with major differences in education, religion, economic status, and political environment. But again, the manner in which the partnership was created shows the power, control, and the interests of the United States in the region and the required changes. Is it for the best for the region?

Is it for the benefit of the West? Is it for both? Questions remain to be answered.

Data Analysis

The analysis shows that in eight out of the nine categories, the official discourse (dominant discourse) has the edge in the frequency of coding (see Figure 3), except for the positive reform code. To give some perspective to the sources of the texts that were analyzed, they included statements from both the G8 and BMENA countries through their official representatives, such as ministers of finance, education, and foreign affairs. The public discourse was produced by civil society organizations that were "chosen" across the BMENA region; they were comprised of academics, lawyers, and other professionals in different fields. However, they do not necessarily claim to represent the population or their individual regions, because only free elections do that.

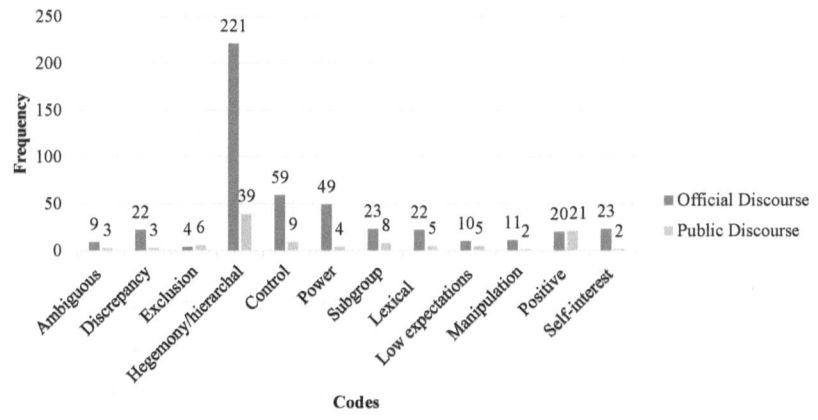

Figure 3. Frequency of codes in both types of discourse

It is important to highlight the difference in the number of documents produced by the partnership, as the total number of documents analyzed was forty-one, only nine of which were produced by civil societies (21.9 percent). If anything, this proportion gives us an indication of discourse control by the G8–BMENA governments. With this in mind, it seems to be a great irony that with this limited access to discourse by the civil society representatives, they evidently were higher in the positive reform category. The positive reform category indicates investment in indigenous knowledge economy, knowledge generation, research, and development. It seems that the officials (G8–BMENA) leaned toward maintaining the status quo of keeping the BMENA region on the consuming end, not that of the producing. The aforementioned figure (figure 3) shows the overall coding system, but each category will be analyzed separately later in the chapter.

As observed, the greatest number of occurrences was in the concept of hegemony and hierarchical, from both official discourse (G8–BMENA) and public discourse (civil societies). This measure showed the interest in maintaining the existing hegemonic relationship, which speaks to the effects of discourse control via mind control. The following excerpt serves as an example of my interpretation of hegemony and the hierarchical nature of the document:

> With these goals in mind, we [G8] *tried to reinvigorate the BMENA process by giving civil society and private sector equal seats at the table with their government counterparts at all BMENA events* [emphasis added], including the Forum, and focused the citizen-government dialogue on specific, country-based collective problem-solving. (2012 G8–BMENA Initiative, 2012, p. 5)

The statement here is by a G8 representative, which showcases the hegemonic and hierarchical interaction, as the G8 is functioning from a superior position in solving conflicts between governments and their civil societies. The G8 controls the scope, defines the issue, and prescribes the remedy to move forward. This is astonishing to me, because it is a local issue in the first place that needs to be dealt with by the government and its people and organizations. The following comment represents the same hegemonic relation but from a different source, civil society.

> We CSOs [civil society organizations] from the region are accused of being too much Western oriented. *Let us be Eastern oriented and bring positive experiences* [emphasis added] from East towards the region. (National Human Rights Committee, 2011, para. 12)

In this excerpt, we notice the representative of a civil society that I hoped would offer a solution from within, but instead offered another version of reliance on other nations to solve the local problems. I do not call for cutting collaborations with other advanced nations, but it is an issue when it is either heading West or East as suggested by the civil society representatives and not within the country in question or at least in the neighboring countries, which in my estimation would help the region to collaborate in local problem-solving.

The following two excerpts show, first, the serious weakness of the partnership and the BMENA region:

> During the opening session of the 7ᵗʰ Forum for the Future, [BMENA representatives] *held Canada accountable for hindering the progress on the final declaration* [emphasis added]. (National Human Rights Committee, 2011, para. 7).

> G8 and Broader Middle East and North Africa
> (BMENA) countries *failed to come up with a joint*
> *declaration with Canada being held responsible for the*
> *failure* [emphasis added]. (National Human Rights
> Committee, 2011, para. 1)

And second, they unwisely illustrate clearly the hierarchical type of relationship the G8 has with the region because one single country, Canada, which does not have a lot of appearance in the BMENA, had the power to cause the failure to the meeting of that year. But again, group power is crystallized in this scenario, because Canada alone cannot deviate from the G8 agenda. Another disappointing fact that speaks to the low expectations of the partnership was the producing of a joint statement probably to score a political point or to improve public relations. Furthermore, twenty-seven BMENA "independent" countries that seek reform cannot produce their own statements without the approval of Canada. Again this shows the superficial kind of partnership at hand. I introduced the negative impact of globalization in chapter 2 that the BMENA region suffers, and again with the following statement, we see the invasion of Western values as if they are a prerequisite part of reform:

> In addition to the educational value of these kinds of
> interventions, participants are exposed to *American*
> *values, culture, and democratic institutions* [emphasis
> added]. (US Department of State, 2008, para. 20)

Also troubling is the wording of "American values, culture"—it makes me wonder which values and culture are referenced. The statement also implies that the local values and culture may prevent the needed progress, which invariably is fallacious in my judgment, because not only is it untrue, but also it causes mental colonization and more self-flagellation. That is because a culture cannot be antithetical to reform and progress. Rather, political and economic circumstances contribute to stagnation.

Power and control are second in the total number of codes, which indicates the gloomy condition of the partnership during the time period of the analyzed documents, 2004–2013. Take, for example, the following statement to illustrate my rationale in coding them as such:

> Furthermore, there are, at present, approximately 90,000 computers in schools, distributed all over the country—a figure, which, according to the Ministry of Education, is expected to increase in the near future. Partners in the Jordanian initiative include: *Cisco Systems, Dell, Hewlett-Packard and France Telecom, amongst others* [emphasis added]. (Office of Her Majesty, Press Department, Dead Sea, 2005, para. 8)

I coded the previous statement as power, control, and self-interest because the G8 has the financial and technological power to provide Jordan with the technology, and I speculate there might be benefits from the effort for Jordan. I am certainly not interested in receiving the computers, but I would have liked to see the computers made in Jordan or any other country in the region. The partnership did not advocate for building Jordan's infrastructure so that the country would be able to invest in local companies to manufacture its own products. The statement shows self-interest because the companies are American and French, and the effort would improve their sales and improve their technologies, not those of Jordan.

Research Findings

My research findings reveal that the analyzed documents of the G8–BMENA Partnership for the years 2004–2013 have nine major themes (codes) and three subthemes (subcodes), which I introduced in table 1. These codes are relevant to my research methodology, critical research analysis, in that they unpack domination and power relations embedded in the documents. The total number of documents analyzed was forty-one. Thirty-two of these documents were produced by official entities, either by the G8 or BMENA officials, and the remainder of the documents were produced by civil society organizations. The purpose of analyzing documents from both types of sources is to investigate where these two types of sources connect and disconnect in the proposed reform.

In the following section, I introduce the meaning of each code, provide the total number of occurrences in both official and public discourse, and also provide excerpts from the documents that represent each code and my reasoning for coding them as such.

Hegemony/Hierarchy

Hegemony/hierarchy is the major theme found in the data, and it focuses on macro-level domination with the consent of the dominated groups (BMENA countries and civil societies). However, in many statements I found evidence of micro-actionable statements that contributed to the macro-level domination, such as financial or political power, which in essence controls the agenda and discussion of the proposed reform that the G8–BMENA is seeking.

The analysis produced 260 statements of hegemonic relationship from both the official discourse and public discourse. The official discourse represents 85 percent (221 occurrences), while the public discourse makes up 15 percent (39 occurrences). The following excerpt published by the G8 research group shows a macro-level domination:

> The Greater Middle East Initiative, *unveiled by the United States* [emphasis added] at the 2004 Sea Island Summit in June, was *motivated by the U.S led desire to stem the threats of political instability* [emphasis added], economic stagnation and terrorism in the Greater Middle East. (Broader Middle East & North Africa Initiative, 2005, p. 11)

This excerpt shows the unilateral action taken by the United States to unveil the partnership, which is a clear indication of a hierarchical relationship between the United States and the entire region. It also highlights the US desire behind the partnership as the most important factor—not what the region actually needs for reform. It is considered hegemonic because the action is taken by the United States, which has the power to unveil the partnership, with no indication that the region has any control over the action or the process. van Dijk (2001b) considers action or process control as a macro-level domination, which is represented in the discourse control. The following figure shows the frequency of macro-hegemonic statements found in both official discourse and public discourse.

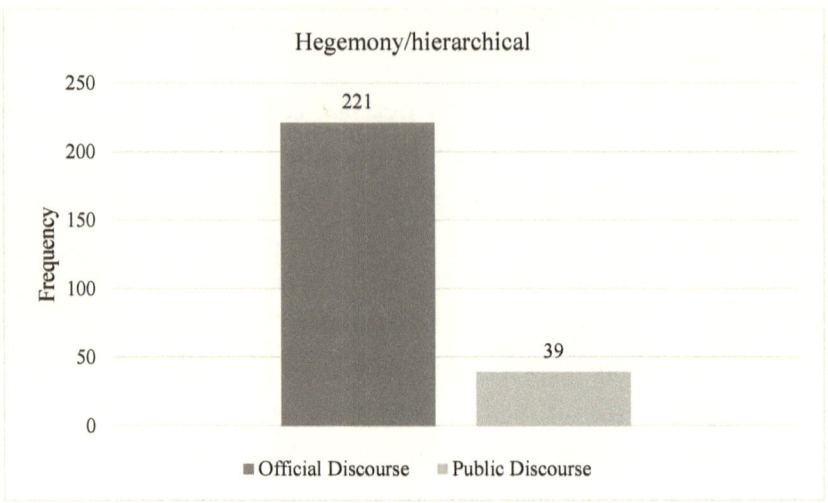

Figure 4. Number of statements coded as hegemonic/
hierarchical relationship observed in the analyzed
documents produced by G8–BMENA and civil societies

Subcodes

As far as the following three subcodes go, they represent a second level (micro) of hegemonic relationship between the G8 and
BMENA countries that appears in both types of discourses (official
and public), and they are characterized by either actionable statements that mean more benefits for the G8 or simply statements
that dictate/impose the outcomes in an overt manner. This is the
reason for having them coded under the umbrella of hegemony
and hierarchy.

Control

Control is defined by concrete actions such as providing financial assistance that in essence would allow the dominant group
to control the agenda of a meeting and the expected outcomes

from the partnership. It also means controlling times and locations of meetings, and membership of countries in the G8–BMENA Partnership. The number of BMENA countries in the partnership was initially twenty-three (Federal Ministry of Education and Research Oman 2005), and by 2012, there were twenty-seven (Chatham House, 2013). The total statements of control were sixty-eight, a figure that appears in all documents from 2004 to 2013. Some 86 percent of control indications were from the official discourse (fifty-nine occurrences), while control was evident in 13 percent of the public discourse (nine occurrences). Here is an example of control in one of the official documents:

> Establish together with our partners a Forum for the Future to:

> Provide a *ministerial framework* [emphasis added] for our on-going dialogue and engagement on political, economic, and social reform in a spirit of mutual respect;

> Bring together in one forum foreign, economic and other ministers of the G-8 and the region *on a regular basis* ... [emphasis added]. (The White House Office of the Press Secretary, 2004, paras. 2)

In the foregoing comment, we observe the official discourse (G8) controlling not only the level of representation (ministers) but also the scope and frequency of discussions, instead of the concerned entity (BMENA) having a free choice, which would be ideal since the reform affects their region, not that of the G8. It a representation of what van Dijk (2001b) highlights about controlling discourse context, which is not limited to controlling meeting times, meeting locations, and who is part of the discourse (membership), but goes further to control ideologies, knowledge, goals, and opinions.

Power

Political, economic, and educational power is represented by G8 advancement in those fields, which essentially portrays the G8 countries as legitimate entities that are entitled to impose their views of reform and to decide what the reform should involve. The alternative would be a scope of reform generated from within the BMENA region.

The analysis shows that power was tagged in the documents fifty-three times. Official discourse produced forty-nine statements, or 92.5 percent, while the public discourse showed fewer power-related statements of only four occurrences or 7.5 percent. Consider, for example, the following statement:

> The United States is *sponsoring* [emphasis added] "partnership schools" to enhance the quality of primary and secondary education, and conducting teacher training and *providing classroom materials* [emphasis added] for early childhood education in Morocco, Tunisia, Oman, and Qatar. (White House Office of the Press Secretary, 2004, para. 97)

This shows the financial power of the United States, which gives it the authority or legitimacy to sponsor a school for a specific purpose (teacher training) and to provide class materials for students. Power here represents hegemonic influence on less powerful countries in the region, which in essence keeps the region on the receiving end by the acceptance of the financial "assistance" and in return keeps the G8 in a position to influence ideology and opinions on the reform. In other words, the financial power will determine the kind of reform, which may not necessarily be real reform that meets the region's needs.

Subgroup

Subgrouping was recorded when there was a conflict between groups internationally (between the G8 and the BMENA countries) or locally (between BMENA countries and civil society organizations). For example, when a government interacted with a civil society organization, I observed a subtle language structure that shows a hierarchical relationship. This can also be considered as othering. The total number of subgrouping (othering) statements was thirty-one. Again, the official discourse produced the majority of subgroupings, with 74.2 percent (twenty-three occurrences), and with 25.8 percent for the public discourse (eight occurrences). Looking at the following two excerpts will showcase this type of interaction:

> With these goals in mind, we tried to reinvigorate the BMENA process by *giving* civil society and private sector *equal seats at the table with their government counterparts at all BMENA events* [emphasis added], including the Forum, and focused the citizen-government dialogue on specific, country-based collective problem-solving. (2012 G8–BMENA Initiative, 2012, p. 5)

> The G-8 could *"encourage the region's governments to allow* [emphasis added] civil society organizations." (*Al Hayat* Arabic newspaper, 2004, para. 12)

This shows hierarchical and hegemonic relationships in an obvious manner, not only between the BMENA and civil societies but also by having the G8 work as a mediator between the two because it has leverage over the two. The comments also show the unequal representation of the civil societies from the inception of this partnership, as they have been othered, and the G8 "attempts" to reconcile the two from a superior position. Figure 5 shows the frequency of the three subcodes and the source of discourse from the analyzed documents.

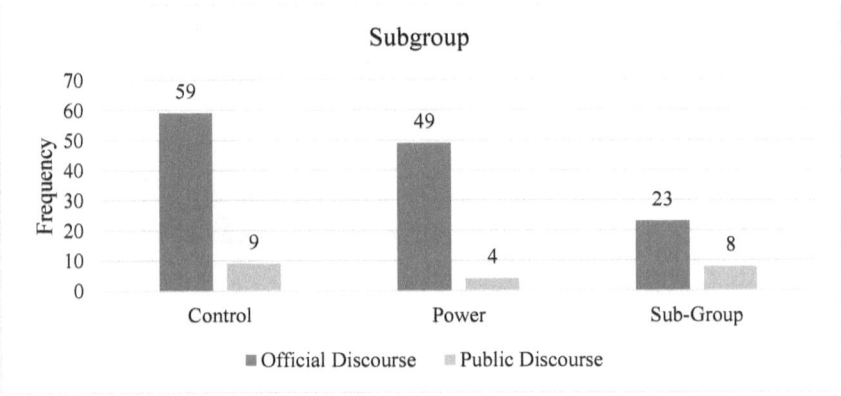

Figure 5. Number of statements coded as control, power, and subgroup (othering) observed in the analyzed documents produced by G8–BMENA and civil societies

Manipulation

Manipulation was recorded in these situations where we see statements by the G8 or BMENA countries made to numb countries, organizations, and people's emotions toward the partnership, making it appear to offer real solutions and hope for reform. Manipulation was tagged thirteen times. Official discourse has eleven occurrences (84.6 percent), while public discourse has only two counts (15.4 percent). Statements were coded under this

category after I found historical background about this partnership and realized that the real intentions behind it were to further
exploit the region economically and politically. The following statement shows a misleading promise:

> We [G8] declare our support for democratic, social
> and economic reform *emanating from that region* [em-
> phasis added]. (White House Office of the Press
> Secretary, 2004, para. 1)

This is just one of many examples that gives the reader the
impression of the region's free will in adopting reforms in governance and socioeconomic spheres and covertly holds the region
responsible for the outcomes (either success or failure). In other
words, if the reform efforts emanating from the region are not
successful, it is the result of the efforts put into the reform by the
region. However, I have established that the partnership was fully
created and designed by the United States with European support
without any consultation with the region (Sharp, 2005), meaning
that it essentially neglected the fundamental needs for progress. I
believe manipulative statements were embedded in the discourse
to brighten the public image of the partnership, and also perhaps
to cause a rift between local populations and their governments.
Figure 6 shows the frequency of the recorded manipulation statements in both types of discourses.

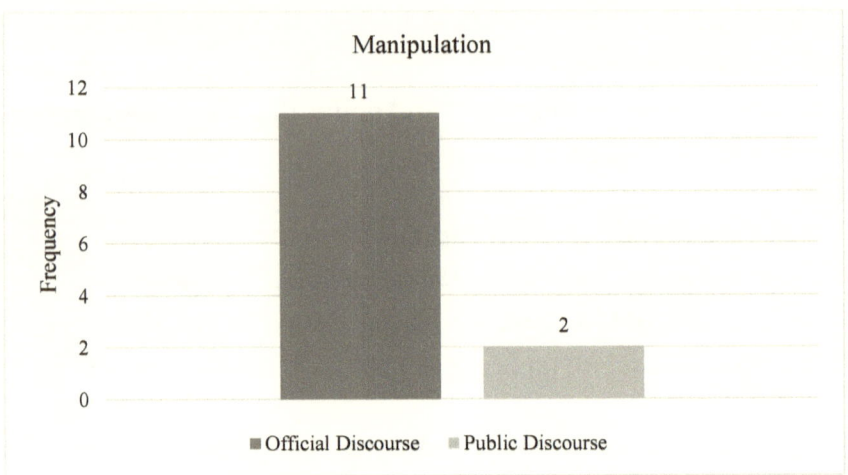

Figure 6. Number of statements coded as manipulation observed in the analyzed documents produced by G8–BMENA and civil societies

Ambiguity

Ambiguous statements were coded in some of the analyzed documents where statements could be interpreted in multiple ways. It is also possible that the statements were intentionally made ambiguous so as to avoid any commitments from the partnership. Ambiguous statements were found twelve times. Again, the official discourse dominated the majority of the statements, with nine occurrences (75 percent), while the statements occurred three times (25 percent) in the public discourse. Consider, for example, the following official statement:

> Ministers affirmed the importance of the continuation of *informal dialogue* [emphasis added]. (2012 G8–BMENA Initiative, 2012, p. 9)

I take issue with the phrase "informal dialogue," because at the end of the day, such statements are not binding. I consider them to be toothless statements because they do not obligate the parties involved to commit to any reform. What makes matters worse is the fact that the informal dialogue is between the representatives of civil societies and, in some cases, includes government officials. It is ambiguous because one wonders about the real reason behind the partnership. How do we expect an already othered low-status group such as a civil society to produce serious reform efforts in an *informal dialogue*? The following figure shows the frequency of the ambiguous statements, along with their sources.

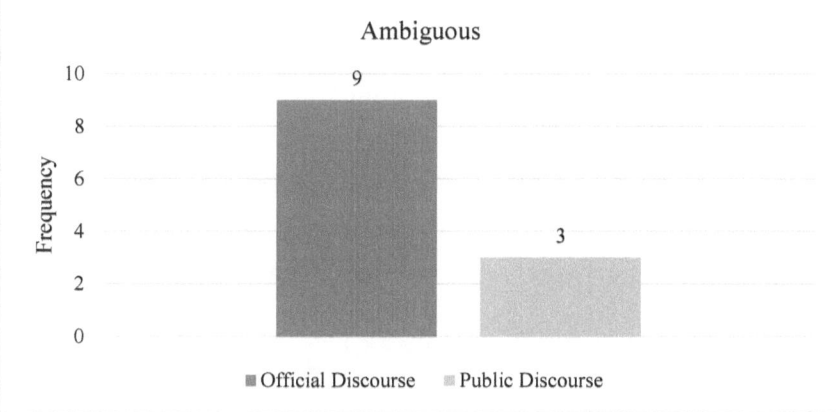

Figure 7. Number of statements coded as ambiguous observed in the analyzed documents produced by G8–BMENA and civil societies

Low Expectations

Some statements were coded as such when I had higher expectations than what the partnership had considered to be an "accomplishment," such as producing a joint declaration or advocating for basic education. The total number of such statements was fifteen, and official discourse yet again was in the lead, producing ten occurrences (66.7 percent). The public discourse had five occurrences (33.3 percent). The following statement clearly shows the low expectation or lack of seriousness in the reform effort:

> At the Forum, *we achieved a historic outcome: a consensus declaration* [emphasis added] (for only the second time in BMENA's nine-year history). (2012 G8–BMENA Initiative, 2012, p. 5)

The phrasing of the sentence is embarrassing, to say the least, especially coming as it does from a governmental entity. The statement was made during the ninth annual meeting, which had been preceded by several meetings, workshops, and trips between countries, costing massive amounts of money, and the historic outcome was "a joint declaration"—not resolving the Arab-Israeli conflict or developing technological capacity in the region. It shows us the low expectations set for the partnership. It seems to me and to some of the civil societies representatives that this partnership is a public relations gathering whose only purpose is to pursue hidden governmental goals while presenting the false hope of helping the region and its people. To put it in perspective, we have thirty-five countries from both the G8 and the BMENA region, and they considered a consensus declaration to be a historic outcome, because it had happened only twice in the life of this partnership. Figure 8 shows the number of low-expectation statements that appear in both types of discourse.

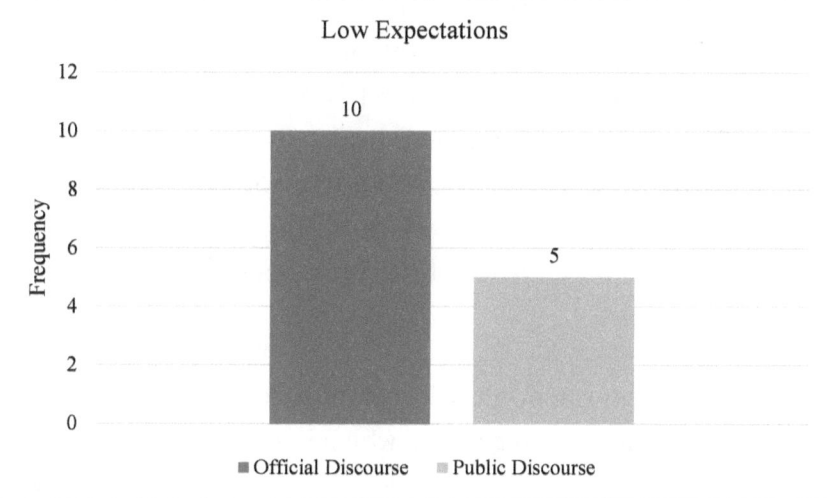

Figure 8. Number of statements coded as showing low expectations observed in the analyzed documents produced by G8–BMENA and civil societies

Self-Interest

The reason for coding something as self-interest was when I believed that the majority of benefits, such as political and economic advantages, were for the G8 countries, not for the BMENA region. However, a self-interest-based action does not deprive the BMENA region from all benefits; indeed it may gain some. But if the partnership is for the region, then the formula needs to be flipped so that BMENA gains the maximum economic, political, and educational benefits, not the G8. Self-interest was observed twenty-five times, twenty-three of which were observed in the official discourse, which equates to 92 percent, while it was produced only two times (8 percent) in the public discourse.

> Promoting financial excellence and supporting efforts in the region to *integrate its financial sector into the global financial system* [emphasis added], including by: providing technical assistance to modernize financial services, and to introduce and expand market-oriented financial instruments. (White House Office of the Press Secretary, 2004, para. 95)

There is a prevalent global economic logic in the statement and in the partnership in general, which is a response to the global demand to have BMENA countries sign free trade agreements (Noi, 2011) mainly for the purpose of opening those countries' markets for the United States and Europe to sell their products. Nevertheless, the BMENA countries will gain minimal benefits compared with those of the G8. It is important to observe the phrasing of the statement "to modernize financial services," which implies that the G8 is tirelessly working for the benefit of the region. Note that—dangerously—nothing is mentioned about the reciprocal nature of these trade agreements. In other words, the region will be obligated to consume more Western products, which will prevent it from establishing its own industries. Figure 9 shows the number of tagged statements that represent more benefits for the G8 countries.

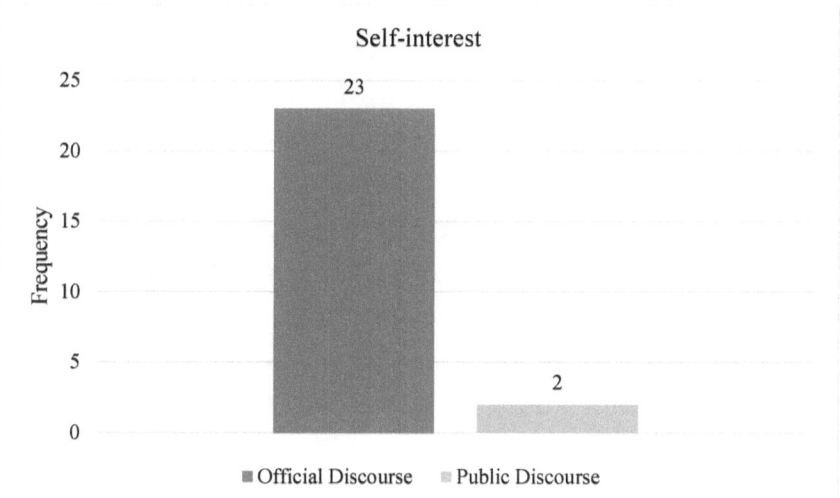

Figure 9. Number of statements coded as showing greater interests for the G8 countries observed in the analyzed documents produced by G8–BMENA and civil societies

Exclusion

Exclusion was coded when it was a higher group that had the power to exclude another group, and this could happen either between the G8 and BMENA countries or between civil societies and BMENA countries. Exclusion was found occasionally (ten times) throughout the data. Official discourse produced four occurrences (40 percent), whereas the public discourse produced six (60 percent). It seems that in the public discourse, civil society representatives were able to document the behavior of either the BMENA or G8 countries, as they often refer to them in a way that shows leverage and lower status. Following is an example of such an interaction:

The representatives of the civil society presented a number of recommendations to the preliminary meeting of the Forum for the Future last September in New York. What became of such recommendations? Were they discussed? What was the stance on them? Did the governments respond to such recommendations? Were some of them adopted? *Or were they "archived"? Up to the moment the civil society did not receive any response!* [emphasis added]. (2012 G8-BMENA Initiative, 2004, p. 2)

This statement by the civil society (public discourse) shows the othering concept and expresses the civil society's frustration. Obviously they are not real partners on an equal footing in the reform efforts. Civil societies conduct their parallel meetings and then submit their recommendations to the official entity, which has the liberty either to address the concerns of the civil societies or not because it is the official entity that controls the final publications and media outlets. This scenario is a crystal-clear representation of discourse control by the dominant group, as van Dijk (2001b) describes in his view of critical discourse analysis. Figure 10 shows the number of coded statements representing exclusion.

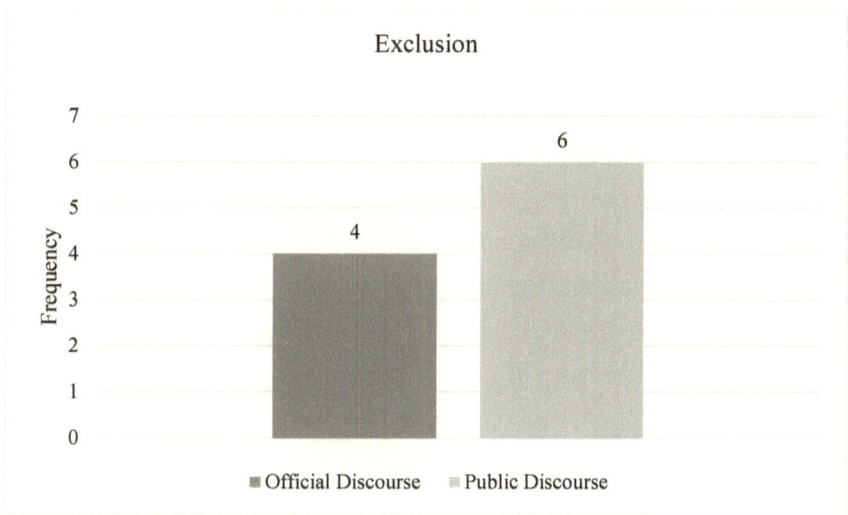

Figure 10. Number of statements coded as exclusionary observed in the analyzed documents produced by G8–BMENA and civil societies

Discrepancy

Discrepancy was coded when there was a mismatch found in statements, in either the official or public discourses, that showed conflict with the overall purpose of the G8–BMENA Partnership, which is to implement educational, political, and socioeconomic reforms. The total number of discrepancies was twenty-five. The official discourse produced the majority of that number, with twenty-two occurrences (88 percent), while the remaining three occurrences were from the public discourse (12 percent). An example of discrepancy is seen in the following text:

> However, due to *tensions between the United States and Egypt* over the arrest of Egyptian opposition party leaders, this *meeting has been postponed* [emphasis added]. (Broader Middle East & North Africa Initiative, 2005, p. 13)

This comment shows how fragile the partnership is. Because of a disagreement over a political issue, the United States has the power to cancel what is supposed to be an important meeting to address extremism and socioeconomic concerns in the region due to the arrest of some opposition leaders, even though the United States has been backing the Egyptian government for decades and has been providing it with financial "support." In other words, the statement shows discrepancy with the overall purpose of reform given that the meeting includes political reform, among other issues, and it was canceled, which in essence does not serve the region in general or the opposition leaders in particular. Figure 11 shows the number of statements that contain discrepancies with the overarching purpose of the partnership.

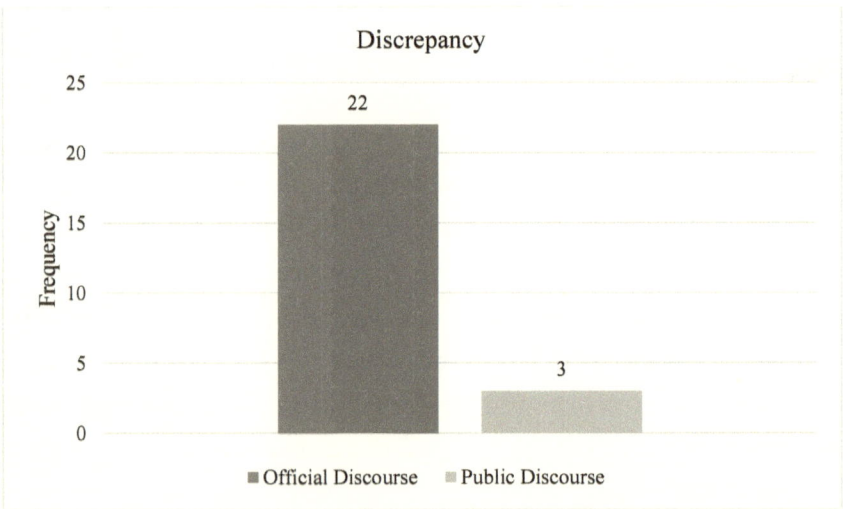

Figure 11. Number of statements coded as discrepant observed in the analyzed documents produced by G8–BMENA and civil societies

Lexical Issues

Lexical issues were coded when I noticed there was an overt or covert indication of superiority or higher power reflected in word choices, which organize groups in a hierarchical fashion. Analyzing lexical structure is an important feature of critical discourse analysis approach (van Dijk, 1997). The number of coded lexical issues was twenty-seven. Official discourse produced the majority of those statements, with twenty-two occurrences (81.5 percent). The public discourse produced five statements (18.5 percent). Following is an Arabic text produced by the United States government that shows the issue:

في ما يلي بيان الحقائق الذي أصدرته وزارة الخارجية الأميركية يوم 20 أيلول/سبتمبر
ويتضمن الخطوط العريضة للمعلومات الأساسية وجدول أعمال الاجتماع
الذي سيعقد في نيويورك [emphasis added]

(US Department of State, 2004, para. 3)

Following is the translation of the quotation that appears in the document:

> Below is a fact sheet issued by the U.S. State Department on September 20 and *it outlines the guidelines and the agenda of the meeting* [emphasis added] to be held in New York. (US Department of State, 2004, para. 3)

In this excerpt, we see a lexical problem in that the partnership does not even try to convey the message covertly, which shows that the United States not only had taken an undisputable charge in deciding when and where the meeting would be held but also had outlined the *guidelines* and the agenda for the meeting for twenty-seven *independent* countries. Figure 12 shows the number of lexical issues found in the documents, along with their sources.

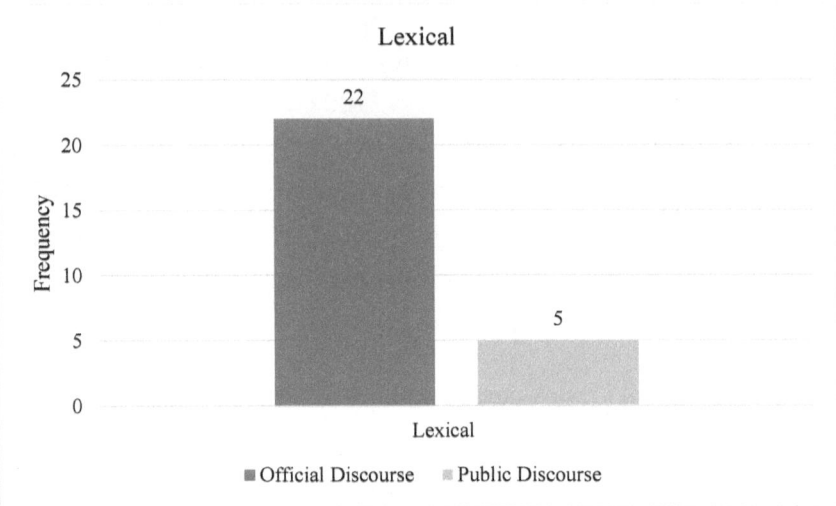

Figure 12. Number of statements coded as exhibiting lexical issues observed in the analyzed documents produced by G8–BMENA and civil societies

Positive Reform

It is not my intention to minimize the positive recommendations or statements produced by all parties involved in the G8–BMENA Partnership, but I have to say that the consideration of a positive or real reform is subjective, because in my understanding, real reform occurs when there is, for example, an agreement on a scientific partnership or an investment in research and development. On the other hand, the G8–BMENA Partnership considers producing a joint declaration or providing classroom materials as a reform or an achievement. Therefore, the positive reform code was applied *only* to statements indicating real reform efforts that match my definition, such as an investment in an indigenous knowledge economy, knowledge creation as opposed to knowledge consumption, or capacity building. With this in mind, positive reform statements were tagged forty-one times. Official discourse produced twenty occurrences (48.8 percent), whereas twenty-one statements are from the public discourse (51.2 percent). The following comment serves as an example of what I consider to be a positive or real reform:

> *Developing a scientific and practical index for measuring the progress of the Arab states* [emphasis added] in the process of reform and issuing an annual report thereon. (2012 G8-BMENA Initiative, 2004, p. 13)

This comment serves as one example of a positive outcome in my analysis, because it is not advocating for reliance on international agencies (e.g., the United Nations) to provide annual progress reports about the status of the region. On the contrary, it seeks to develop a local agency that analyzes the status of the Arab countries in the scientific field. It is a natural progression, starting with a needs assessment (deficiency), and then moving forward to create locally inspired and locally developed solutions for those deficiencies. The following figure shows the number of coded positive reform statements and their sources.

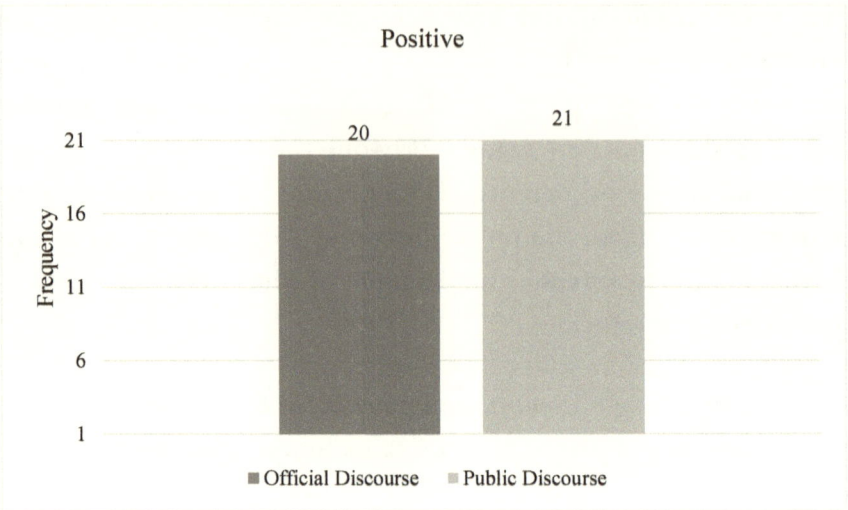

Figure 13. Number of statements coded as positive (real reforms) observed in the partnership documents produced by G8–BMENA and civil societies

Educational Discourse

It is of paramount importance for this research to demystify the underlying agenda for the G8–BMENA Partnership and its annual meetings. I achieved that end through analyzing official documents generated by the governments from both the G8 and the BMENA regions, with some input from civil societies. The scope of reform in the partnership includes three major areas: educational, economic, and social. It is important to highlight the main reason for this partnership. It was launched to counter extremism emanating from the BMENA region that threatens peace and stability, not only in the region but also in the world, and in particular the United States.

In the wake of 9/11, many nations collaborated to face the evil threat not only to the West but also to the region, and what makes matters worse is that those extremists hijacked Islam for their own twisted agenda and found global media that gave them an avenue to spread fear. Under the banner of war on terror, along with the political and economic alliances that have been created, education has to be addressed. I do not disagree with that premise, but I do disagree with the agenda and the manner in which this partnership was created.

Two types of discourse emerged, (a) education for the labor market (material) and (b) security or political discourse (rhetorical), which in essence created a new hegemonic relationship between the G8 (the United States in particular) and the BMENA countries, which were represented covertly in institutional and professional domination. This speaks to the domination shift from overt coercive group domination to something more subtle (Danet, 1984; O'Barr et al., 1978; Bradac et al., 1981; Ng & Bradac, 1993; Wodak, 1984), where it appears legitimate because of the global threats we all face. So, how does the double-edged sword of hegemony appear in the G8–BMENA Partnership? We already know who had control and power in creating the entire partnership. Not only that, the analysis shows the G8 control over the agenda, scope, region, countries, agreements, and declarations, along with the G8's ability to deem any outcomes to be either a success or a failure. And finally, we know about the G8 benefits of selling educational materials and curriculum to the BMENA region. These arrangements usually are carried out by international organizations and NGOs that publicize information to influence international agendas for reform. Lingard (2000) states the following in this regard:

> The effects of globalization on the state, education policy, and schools are mediated yet again by local cultures, histories, and politics. Globalization maps onto local practice in contingent, contested, inflected, and thus unpredictable ways. (p. 102)

Globalization comes with contestation as a main characteristic. When looking at the forty-one documents, we find that the majority of them address the labor market and its connection to education (material), which now has created a global logic to incorporate the private sector as a major partner in educational reform. The influence of this connection between education and the private sector is seen in the policies developed by the BMENA. Therefore, there is a conflict between the global and the local logics, but the weight of the global logic has more influence thanks to the funding resources allocated to it and the political power that supports it.

It is observed time and again that the reform includes teacher training and basic education curriculum (BEC), which includes teaching English language as a life skill. The issue here is that these elements are closely tied to the labor market to create more jobs, but the real focus should be on education as liberation from local and Western domination. In other words, BEC advocates for a narrow educational philosophy, which may provide a short-term objective, as opposed to an educational view that addresses larger issues such as political exploitation, social stratification, and a dominant economic model. The partnership does not advocate to reform fundamental issues that contribute to the region's stagnation, such as social justice and equity, but rather it advocates for capitalism and a neoliberal educational agenda, which in essence keeps the region dependent on the G8 for its political and economic stability. I must point out that this could not have happened without local support, whether conscious or unconscious.

Language Use in G8–BMENA Meetings

Globalization and hegemony use a certain rhetoric of "soft governance." Dale (1999) believes that they use noncoercive and discursive techniques to gain confidence and buy-in from governments.

This appears to be the case in the G8–BMENA Partnership through their collaboration in two major areas:

I. Labor market and its relation to education
    o   creating partnerships with the private sector
    o   teacher training
    o   entrepreneurship
II. Perceptions and language use
    o   best practices
    o   relevance of education
    o   education's relationship to prosperity
    o   targets

These premises are representative of a dominant global understanding, which defines education and its purpose in a society, and also defines development and what it looks like. However, the G8–BMENA recommendations were not created in the BMENA region, and they may conflict with the local vision or understanding of reform. Lawn (2006) indicates that a soft governance approach would use soft tools such as conferences, seminars, and advisory groups to rally the target audience, which is the case with the partnership at hand.

When the partnership discusses educational, social, and economic reform, we have to understand that the political context in the G8 that generates the agenda for the BMENA region is utterly disconnected from the region it supposedly wants to help. Therefore, when reading the documents and discussions between G8 ministers and their BMENA counterparts, we notice that they almost speak two different languages, because their priorities are different. An example is when Canada blocked a joint declaration in an annual meeting because there was a disagreement on the major obstacle in the face of any kind of reform and, I may add, world peace: the conflict between Palestine and Israel. In other words, the G8 was focusing on the symptoms of the issue but not on the issue itself. Take, for example, the following statement by the minister of foreign affairs of the United Arab Emirates:

لا يمكنكم أن تأتوا إلى المنتدى وتتكلموا مع المنطقة وتقولوا نحن نتناول فقط الأمور التي نريد أن نتناولها ولا نريد تناول الأمور التي تريدون انتم تناولها، أي شيء اقل مما جاء في البيان الرئاسي للمنتدى في المغرب عام ٢٠٠٩ لن نقبل به

(Farhat, 2011, para. 21)

Following is the translation of the foregoing quotation that appeared in the document:

> You cannot come to the forum and engage in a dialogue with the region and say we are dealing only with the issues that we want to deal with, and refuse to discuss the issues that we want to address, anything less than what came in the presidential statement of the Forum in Morocco in 2009, will not be accepted. (Farhat, 2011, para. 21)

As far as educational reform goes, I draw from a great analogy that Kaldor (1981) made to address the baroque arsenal (not advanced weaponry). In times of peace, weapons making nations gain many benefits, such as money, jobs, infrastructure, success, expansion, and development, by selling these weapons elsewhere while consuming nations remain in their lagging positions if not falling behind since they are losing their wealth and eventually face their demise. This scenario can apply to educational reform suggested by the partnership. When the G8 (center) transfers "best practices," education models, curriculum, institutions, and accreditations to the BMENA region (periphery), it takes years for those things to be received and implemented. With this in mind, the region will receive outdated products, "a baroque educational arsenal," not only designed in a different environment and by a different culture but also delivered years later, which in essence may hinder any possibility of building local infrastructure. This will cause the region continue to slip farther behind on a global level, will continue to strain the national resources of the BMENA countries, and will also benefit the G8 countries on many levels. This shows the relationship between the center and the periphery, where the "centers grow stronger and more dominant and the peripheries become increasingly marginalized" (Altbach, 2006, p. 24).

I am not suggesting that establishing best practices and monitoring, accreditation, and quality assurance agencies is a bad idea, but I think these things fall under the category of secondary issues for the BMENA region. I believe the real concern is the mental control (colonization) that either causes the region to fail to be productive in developing indigenous knowledge economy or actively and intentionally blocks the region from "real" development. This has transpired; look only at the apparent dependence on the G8 in all areas of reform. One would ask: When will the cycle end? The situation of the BMENA is unbelievable. These countries mainly consume outdated knowledge, among other products, and the partnership ironically suggests increasing the number of student scholarships to the West and suggests that students do community service in the West, not in their homelands where the help is needed most, as stated in this statement: "[Students] perform community service while in the United States, and have the opportunity to take part in a number of enhancement activities designed to heighten their awareness of civic responsibility and leadership" (US Department of State 2008, para. 23). It also worsens the brain drain situation the region suffers from, as the (United Nations Development Program, 2002) report indicates that 51 percent of adult Arabs show interest in emigrating to the West.

The analysis shows the role of the hegemons in the BMENA region, consisting of key players not only from the G8 but also from within, who have the ability to lobby for support and to participate in creating plans, creating agendas, defining problems, and recommending solutions that may or may not achieve the wanted outcome for the entire BMENA region or individual states. Ritzer (1996) talks about the idea of McDonaldization of higher education, which means offering similar courses, qualifications, training courses, and even quality control in establishments. Some may argue that the burger may travel well, but the same principle does not apply to educational or social reforms. Altbach (2006) highlights the role of universities in modern societies, regardless of location, as the place where locals debate controversial issues that affect their region. Altbach advocates for keeping them independent from local or international hegemonic entities if they are to result in successful outcomes. Therefore, when looking at the role of the G8–BMENA Partnership and the real role of a university, we see conflict, because the G8 focuses on the labor market (material) issues, whereas universities should function as an avenue for a cultural discourse that stems from critical engagement with local issues.

The analysis shows some agreements on transactions for curricula delivery from the G8 to the BMENA region, which showcases an exchange of material and money, but this does not mean an exchange of ideas. That is to say, without real commitment to long-term scientific partnership or collaboration, without capacity building in research and development, reform will not occur in the region. In addition, the region will not be able to contribute to the world knowledge economy, and the region might remain in a relationship characterized by being a recipient of programs and degrees created elsewhere. The alternative scenario would allow the region to be creative in helping the rest of the world tackle common problems facing humanity.

It is important to clarify my position on the economic development and labor market needs in the region. I believe they are an important aspect in societies' stability and advancement. But the issue in this research is knowledge ownership and production. Robertson et al. (2007) address the philosophy of learning, saying that it rests in the ability to develop new capacities that would bridge the learning divide between the West and the "Rest." Development and education reform for that matter rely on the innovation approach that gives the BMENA region the ability to practice with new ideas and technologies with the aim in mind of the region's beginning to develop its own capacity. If we look, for example, at the four following pillars recognized by the World Bank (2003) as the cornerstones for knowledge society— (1) information and infrastructure, (2) economic incentive and institutional regime, (3) innovation systems, and (4) education and learning—we realize these pillars are lacking in the G8–BMENA Partnership.

A knowledge society is primarily dependent not on physical abilities but rather on the use of ideas and the application of technologies. That is to say, a knowledge society follows a cycle that starts with knowledge creation, acquiring that knowledge, and ends with the transmission of and usage of the knowledge by individuals or organizations. Essentially, "the knowledge economy is transforming the demands of the labor market in economies throughout the world" (World Bank, 2003, p. 1). This position flips the current arrangement between the labor market and education, where we put knowledge economy at the heart of any reform, allowing the educational apparatus to inform the labor market, not the other way around.

Another important observation that cannot be ignored is the fact that of the data collected for this research, only one of the forty-one documents analyzed was published in Arabic, and the rest were published in English. Keep in mind that the majority of the BMENA countries have Arabic as their native language. This is ironic, because the reform is about the region, and the official language used in the annual meetings is English. That is just one tool of controlling the official and public discourse. van Dijk (1996) stresses to pay attention to this aspect when we analyze power and domination in talk and text. This also highlights how the G8–BMENA Partnership is actively marginalizing the very population that it is supposedly intending to help, by using a foreign language and ignoring the importance of the native language to its people on so many levels, as was elaborated on in chapter 2.

Political Discourse

The G8–BMENA Partnership did not emerge from a vacuum, but as mentioned, it was created after the 9/11 tragedy, or at least this was the official reasoning espoused by the United States. We cannot analyze its foundation without looking at preceding events in the region, especially the illegal invasion of Iraq. The invasion of Iraq damaged the credibility of the US efforts at "reform" before it even started, or to say the least, it limited the support from the region and from the major European allies. Furthermore, it weakened international law because of the unilateral action taken by the United States in the war (Girdner, 2004). In other words, the show of military power diminished or harmed the political power deployed in the G8–BMENA Partnership. Erhan (2005) claims that there was no real agreement among the G8 countries regarding the planned goals for the BMENA Partnership. Therefore, the initiative remained covertly a US-led project, and this is one of the reasons for its unsuccessful outcome in promoting democracy, human rights, good governance, freedom, and prosperity, considering for the sake of argument that those are the real objectives for the partnership. Europe maintained public relations with the United States by providing superficial political support, which is a representation of group power and domination thorough professional institutions, as illustrated by van Dijk (2001b).

The name of the partnership was initially Greater Middle East (GME), which was met by great suspicion in the region because it echoed previous efforts to create a New Middle East. An article by a retired American colonel titled "Blood Borders," published in the *American Armed Forces Journal* (2006), includes a changed map of the region, which reflects the hidden intention of the United States for the region. That intent was not aligned with the declared promise of the G8–BMENA Partnership. According to the map, there will be changes to the current boundaries of the BMENA countries that were maliciously created by the colonizers in the first place to insure instability. The countries that win more territories are Afghanistan, the Arab Shia State, Armenia, Azerbaijan, Free Baluchistan, Free Kurdistan, Iran, the Islamic Scared State, Jordan, Lebanon, and Yemen. The losers are Afghanistan, Iran, Iraq, Israel, Kuwait, Pakistan, Qatar, Saudi Arabia, Syria, Turkey, the United Arab Emirates, and the West Bank (see Figure 14). According to Nazemroaya (2006) and Peters (2006), the United States claims the map does not reflect the Pentagon's vision for the region, although the map was used for training in the NATO Defense College, the National War Academy, and other military planning circles. Such information could limit any possible success of the partnership, in addition and most importantly the fact that the change is imposed by the United States, neglecting the internal dynamics and the necessity for reform that stems from within.

Figure 14. Middle East and North Africa map. The purpose of this map is to show the location of the countries and their current boundaries. Find more information about the altered map in the reference section.

The analysis shows the following major weaknesses, from a political angle, that characterize the G8–BMENA Partnership:

- A one-size-fits-all approach in a very diverse region, in addition to its prescriptive nature in a very untrusting political climate.
- Lack of coordination with other programs that "aspire" to achieve similar goals, such as the European Mediterranean Partnership (EMP). This partnership will be discussed briefly in the next section.
- The G8–BMENA Partnership was drafted and created in the United States, without consultation with the region.
- The serious weakness was about the Arab-Israeli conflict, which I believe to be the major obstacle for any reform on all levels because it provides a breeding ground for extremism and delays any developmental and reform efforts.

The analysis shows distrust between the two major powers (the United States and European countries) who have many inserts in the region, for example, political, security, and economic inserts, among others, which ultimately caused the failure of the G8–BMENA Partnership. The United States used a rapid transformation in the region via its military power (the 2003 Iraq War), and then used BMENA as another vehicle for transformation (political power). Europe, on the other hand, used a more gradual transformation approach when it created EMP.

One may wonder that because the EMP, led by the European Union and G8–BMENA, led by the United States, agreed on the main principles to reform the region educationally, economically, and socially, would they have more commonality than differences? Are the G8–BMENA and the EMP competing with or complementing each other's efforts? It is a sad reality, mainly because the region seems to be an object controlled by different actors for either common or different purposes, and both the EMP and G8–BMENA claim that their project is for the benefit of the region. Has the region lost its agency in reforming itself? Is the region so weak as to be objectified by both Europe and the United States?

The BMENA and EMP partnerships may have a lot in common with respect to the future of the region, but there is evident competition between the two. Noi (2011) sheds light on the divergent political, security, and economic concerns between the United States and Europe. We see the competition in several instances, as discussed in Noi's work:

- Madrid Middle East Peace Conference 1991, where the United States kept pushing Europe away from the process to prevent it from having any political role in the conflict.
- Europe and the United States diverging on the US policy of isolation and containment under the Iran and Libya Sanctions Act, and Europe was involved in dialogue with Iran, which opposed the US policy at the time.
- Europe initiating the Barcelona Process without inviting the United States.
- The US unilateral war in Iraq, which negatively impacted European states and divided them.
- Launching the G8–BMENA Partnership by the United States without real consultation with Europe or without using the existing EMP, which had been founded nine years earlier.
- A superficial involvement of Europe in the G8–BMENA Partnership.

The economic factor intensified the competition between the United States and the EU and their partnerships to control the region, which can be seen in some of the statements found in the BMENA-analyzed documents, as follows:

Turkey is providing technical assistance to facilitate the implementation *of free trade agreements, including training on WTO issues* [emphasis added]. (2012 G8-BMENA Initiative, 2012)

Improved business climates and *open and free trade economies* [emphasis added]. (2012 G8–BMENA Initiative, 2009, p. 17)

... EU to launch discussions on Deep and *Comprehensive Free Trade Agreements* [emphasis added]. (2012 G8–BMENA Initiative, 2011, p. 4)

The wording of these statements may show that the G8 is consumed with the economic reform in the region, but frankly, the fallacy of free trade, open markets, and privatization seems only to open the region's market to sell goods produced in the United States and Europe. This is the main reason for the competition between the two major powers, which ultimately resulted in the failure of the BMENA Partnership. Noi (2011) shows such evidence in the free trade agreements (FTA) established by the United States with some BMENA countries, and in the FTA that Europe established with the Mediterranean and Middle East countries. We may not see with the naked eye the depth and the efforts that took place in planning and establishing such partnerships just by reading final declarations from the BMENA, but now we may because we have analyzed other sources that address the historical background of the region and the context in which these partnerships emerged. This is why analyzing the discursive and historical context is a hallmark of critical discourse analysis, as stressed in the work of Fairclough and Wodak (1997) and van Dijk (2001a).

CHAPTER 5

Discussion

In this concluding chapter, I address the research problem, and the purpose, significance, major results, research implications, and direction for future research. The research problem at hand is that periphery countries around the world, and especially for this research the Broader Middle East and North Africa (BMENA) region, do not have free will to embark on political, educational, or economic reforms, which results in social conditions and ramifications that impede developments in the region. My data analysis shows that the main reason for unsuccessful reform efforts is the multiple levels of hegemony and special interests of the dominant groups, both in the G8 and the BMENA. In other words, I discovered two layers of domination: First, the G8 dominated the BMENA representatives and populations, and second, the BMENA representatives dominated the civil societies and the public, resulting in a trickle-down domination effect.

The purpose of the research was to establish a deep understanding of educational, political, and social challenges facing Saudi Arabia in its foundation and then to use that understanding as an example for my targeted region of analysis, BMENA. I moved to investigate globalization and its challenges in the realm of education, society, and economy, asserting that global Western powers shaped not only the Saudi context but also the entire BMENA region. Moreover, this analysis showed that the partnership is influencing the region's reform today. It was my interest to include an important tool used by globalization, the English language, which has many damaging effects in the region.

From this analysis, it is evident that critical research is limited in the region because of the small number of regional resources, the small number of publications in Arabic, and the local critical researchers whom I was able to have access to. Therefore, the significance of my study relies, first and foremost, on the contribution to the resistance discourse in both the Saudi context and the BMENA region in general. The research also provides a counternarrative to the dominant discourse stemming from either official or public entities that favor in a larger sense the status quo. I do not believe that the partnership attempted to seriously engage in long-lasting developments, but instead offered temporary solutions to permanent problems.

The research questions below have guided me in addressing serious concerns in the BMENA region. They tackle educational, economic, and social problems that are in desperate need of reform.

1. How has the G8 and the Broader Middle East and North African (BMENA) Partnership affected and shaped educational and social reforms in the region since its establishment in 2004?

2. What type of discourse was deployed to perpetuate hegemonic and hierarchical relationships that sustain unequal status between the G8 and BMENA countries?

3. How do the G8 representatives control the BMENA public discourse?

4. How does such discourse control the minds and the actions of people of the BMENA countries, and what are the social consequences of such control?

These questions also investigated the role of G8–BMENA as an international professional institution that promised to generate a reform that came from within the targeted region and was not affected by external influence. Furthermore, I attempted to unpack techniques that the G8 used to rally BMENA governments to be part of reform efforts in their region. It is important to note that my analysis did not paint the region's representatives as victims but rather as responsible participants in the generated outcomes or lack thereof by both being actively and passively involved in this partnership. Moreover, the study discussed the types of discourses generated in this partnership and examined who and what controlled the discourse, what techniques were used, and the consequences of such control. These questions have been addressed in chapter 4. I will address them concisely in this chapter in the Closing Remarks section.

Levels of Hegemony

In order for me to understand hegemony in the region, I needed to dissect the concept of hegemony into layers, relying on my understanding of research by Gramsci (2000), Apple (1990), and Bourdieu (1977). The result gave me the knowledge to divide hegemony in the region into three levels, which I believe will help me in my future work in the realms of domination, power relations, and reproduction. I do not claim that these levels are completely isolated, but rather they are intertwined. The first level of hegemony was observed in my initial review, which I called level one or micro hegemony. I consider it as such because it was internal, within a country, such as Saudi Arabia (chapter 2). It appeared in my research when the Saudi government, at its foundation, used the most sacred tool—the religion of Islam—for the people in achieving its needed political outcome by establishing the country in 1932. The government represented itself as the true representative of the *pure* version of the faith (Unitarian) and therefore domesticated the people so as to achieve that purpose with the consent of the masses. It is considered a hegemonic relationship between the government and the people because the unification of the land does not necessarily represent a unification of the hearts and minds of all people with diverse backgrounds. It also did not result in equality or equity on a wide range of issues.

Education was a major domain for competition between the government and the religious establishment in the Saudi example, and therefore a coalition was made to impose a political and a social agenda, which created an oligarchical ruling system (Abir, 1988). The two parties created a twofold educational system (traditional and secular) to establish their legitimacy and to impose their views, at the cost of education quality, infrastructure, equity, and upward social mobility. This was present in one dominant view of education and religion, ignoring different cultural backgrounds and understandings under the banner of unifying the country, and people largely accepted the premise. It is not a new phenomenon; we observe the rhetoric now in the war on terror. Dominant groups usually use scare tactics to rally populations behind special causes. I found that level one of hegemony is not limited to internal forces, as local hegemons join forces with foreign powers when they have a common goal or when their interests meet, at the expense of the advancement of the local population. However, hegemony here did not represent itself as such but rather used a discourse that disguised the real intentions, using patriotism as a vehicle. This created a sense of parochial nationalism, which added local conflicts, such as tribalism and regionalism, saddled with a rentier economy.

The second level of hegemony (macro) was found in this study when there were clear international political, educational, and economic interests in the region. It is a macro-level domination that showed obvious power in different fields, a scenario that forced weak nations to join coalitions or sign treaties. Globalization from above is the catalyst for this type of hegemony; it affects societies in two major ways, either by homogenizing them or heterogenizing them. I established that adhering to one or the other is not the right reaction to this power, because we need to analyze globalization dialectically. Globalization, as was established in chapter 2, has economic, educational, and cultural dimensions. Furthermore, globalization comes in two forms: First, there is globalization from above, and in this sense it supports domination and exploitation of others; and second, there is globalization from below, where it helps activists to resist globalization by using its tools. This is the dialectic nature of globalization: it can empower and oppress individuals or nations simultaneously.

The third level of hegemony is an ideological one—and I consider it the most dangerous because it is self-imposed. To be more specific, it is a result of mind control by people in power, where the dominated people consent to domination and consider it necessary for their success. It was observed in this study in educational choices made in the Saudi example in establishing modern education, or on the global level in adopting English as the language of science and the language of the world. It is portrayed in this view as a natural phenomenon, not as a man-made phenomenon, which could be rectified. English dominated both the official discourse and the public discourse in the analyzed documents. In other words, I depict this type of hegemony as if marginalized people's consciousness is functioning as an independent agent for domination and reproduction. It seems that marginalized people in many places, and especially in the BMENA region, are unconsciously accepting a lower status because this is the only status they know, and therefore they do not produce an alternative. Moreover, it appears that there is a consciousness conflict; one is seeking independence, freedom, and the ability to decide for oneself, and the other becomes repressed swiftly by unconsciousness or by false consciousness. Figure 15 demonstrates my understanding of hegemony levels that emerged from this study. It is important to note that they are connected; my research showed that each level is supported by the other. Questions that emerge about these levels of hegemony are: What level should we tackle first? Shall we start with the most dangerous (ideological) as a top-down approach, or shall we begin bottom-up? These questions remain to be answered in future research.

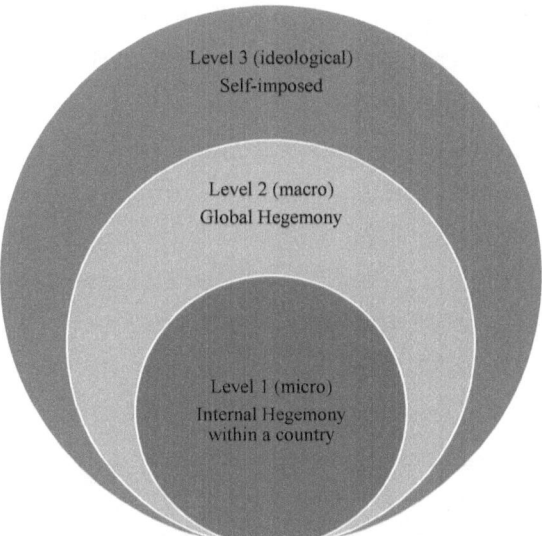

Figure 15. Levels of hegemony observed in the G8–BMENA Partnership

Theoretical Implications

In both the official discourse (dominant) and the public discourse, the concept of hegemony was prevalent, producing the highest number of codes in my analysis. I consider this type of hegemony as level three. It is mental and ideological in that officials and representatives of civil societies relied on imported solutions for local problems. That is to say, the G8 government officials wanted to maintain their control over the discourse, which essentially controls the outcomes, options, and opinions of both BMENA officials and civil society representatives. Not only that, but also BMENA officials and civil society representatives became part of this partnership for different reasons, which evidently did not come to fruition in the needed reform and did not improve the relationship between them. Here, I consider a potential good response to this global power represented in the G8 by using the concept of globalization from below. It gives the region the necessary tools (internet, email, transportation, social media, etc.) provided by globalization from above to create a peaceful regional movement that aligns itself with globalization as hybridization (Pieterse, 1994), which would unify the region against the current dominant model. This dominant model has widened the gap not only between the center and the periphery but also between different classes in the BMENA societies, in the quality of education and in social mobility.

I believe the BMENA region has an identity crisis caused not only by the effects of globalization, because humans have always been global and lived side by side. I realized from this research that the region needs to engage in a process of constructing an identity to create a meaning for itself so that it may generate reform options emanating from within. This process of identification entails a necessary system of difference (self vs. other), which is an important part of constructing an identity. It is a dialectical process that includes self–other (differences–similarities). On one hand, the region needs to identify what makes it different, and on the other hand, it needs to identify what it has in common with the others. Both of these things will allow it to construct its own identity. This comes with a caveat: we must not overemphasize the differences and neglect the similarities, because it is a dialectical system of differences and similarities, and excessive emphasis on one will cause malfunction. It is a balanced approach that recognizes the differences (multiplicity of others) while at the same time finds similarities.

Based on the data analysis, the G8–BMENA was the dominant group that controlled the discourse, as was evident by, first, the number of documents produced and, second, the frequency of codes added in eight of nine categories. The exception was the positive reform category, in which the public discourse was slightly higher (49 percent vs. 51 percent). It was surprising to me that both the official discourse and the public discourse were more connected than disconnected by having more in common in their views regarding educational, economic, and social reforms. I came to the research with an impression that the official discourse (that of the BMENA countries) would be more reliant on the G8 countries in this partnership and thought that the public discourse (civil societies) would be seeking more local solutions to local problems. Unlike what I had expected, both adhered to the G8 agenda without any real active involvement in its creation, and they were passively on the receiving end. To add insult to injury, the G8 was functioning from a superior position as an arbitrator. In many instances, the BMENA representatives met only with the civil societies when the G8 representatives were present. The alternative would have been a meeting between the two local parties where they solved issues together. It is like when the US Congress is gridlocked. We do not expect Europe to intervene, let alone the BMENA region to bridge the gap between Democrats and Republicans, because at the end of the day it is a local American issue and it has to be solved locally without major foreign influence. In addition, Europe was minimally involved in the partnership for one reason or another, but my analysis showed that the reason for its involvement was to maintain the power and control of the Western group over the region in a superficial collaboration with the United States.

I believe both the official discourse and the public discourse fall under the third level of hegemony described above, which represents mental colonization and false consciousness stemming from decades of colonization and which now is under another project known as globalization. This consciousness is considered false when it perpetuates the status quo of domination and inequality and when it makes a subordinate group (or countries, in this study) lose its agency to determine its future. False consciousness made these countries incapable of taking action against the causes of their subordination. Cunningham (1987) refers to false consciousness as "harbouring of false beliefs that sustain one's own oppression" (p. 255); that is why this level of hegemony is the most dangerous in my analysis. The BMENA region is involved in the globalization project, whether willing or unwillingly, to maintain the superstructure of the world (hierarchy), where the West remains at the top and the Rest occupy a lower status. The top of the hierarchy seems to exert what is necessary to remain in that position by compromising with the G8 countries (group power) to achieve a common goal of political and economic exploitation. In other words, the game remains the same, but the rules change to serve a similar purpose. For example, game-changing tactics appear when we see domination shift from a hard power (military) to a soft power (political) through establishing professional institutions and partnerships, because these institutions project a facade of genuine interest in the well-being of the region. Keep in mind that the partnership produced only two joint declarations (low expectations), and when the region pushed for addressing the single political issue (the Arab-Israeli conflict) that caused all of the deterioration and extremism in the region, Canada was responsible for the failure of the seventh annual meeting. It is important to note that the region pushed for political reform for this issue adhering to UN Security Council Resolutions 242 and 338 (Secretary Powell and Moroccan Foreign Minister Benaissa, 2004), which was again created by the major powers, and nonetheless the resolution was ignored by the major powers. It makes me wonder: Is the partnership intended to maintain the conflict, as senseless as this sounds, so as to give the major powers leverage and access to maintain power and control over the region?

Social Implications

I claim that the social ramifications are many, the first one being the maintaining of a culture of dependency in almost all aspects of life—educational, economic, political, and social—because, as represented in the analysis, only a fraction of the reform suggested advocated for local solutions. I have been led to believe that the partnership has worsened the Arabic mentality because of Arab states' continued reliance on Western models and points of view. These views were reproduced in the partnership by local elites—or what I referred to in chapter 2 as the transnational class, because they have more in common with the elites in New York or London than with their own people. This created a chain reaction. If people in BMENA want to move up in society, they must adapt to the dominant global logic and the global way of thinking, which represents an ideological work that seems to gain strength, and some consider it to be unstoppable.

Second, only one of the forty-one documents that were gathered and analyzed in this project was published in Arabic. I considered the spread of the English language to be a major issue in chapter 2 because Arabic is the native language of most countries in the region. I consider the absence of publications in Arabic as alienation of the very people and the region the G8 is trying to "reform." It is the neoliberal story that portrays English as a neutral tool and as a transparent language (Pennycook, 1994) for international communication to make it less threatening to the 75 percent of the world population who either do not speak the language or for whom it is a second or foreign language. Here we see an alignment between this view of English and the view of globalization as a natural phenomenon.

It is a perfect representation of Gramsci's (2000) understanding of cultural hegemony observed in the portrayal of the English language as a tool. If it is a tool, then people rationalize its necessity in international communication, and in turn, English does not threaten their linguistic, national, or ethnic identities if we do not engage in its historical background. In other words, it reinforces the English language's powerful position with the consent of the BMENA officials and the civil societies' representatives, forgetting that it is an imposed language, which limits involvement from the people most affected who undeniably are in need of reform.

However, the position of the English language needs to be looked at dialectically, because first, when organizations "choose" English as a medium of communication, this sometimes empowers activists and researchers in the context of globalization from below. This is because it provides them the opportunity to rally international activists and critical thinkers from around the world to bring an international perspective to a common issue, and it provides access to resources and information. Second, using English could also oppress people in that it can alienate the majority of those who do not have the language capital. Therefore, we need to look at the English language through a lens of oppression and empowerment, because if we look at it only from the empowerment dimension, we obscure its hegemonic role in a society, and if we look at it from a dimension of oppression and reject it, we lose its potential to support globalization from below. At the end of the day, English is a reality in our lives, but if it has to be taught, it should be taught in a critical way that empowers its users and not be made a prerequisite for advancement at all levels.

Political Implications

My analysis unexpectedly revealed a greater political challenge facing the region. As stated previously in the research, educational, economic, and social issues are hard to precisely isolate because those domains influence each other greatly. However, through the critical lens I used in analyzing the documents, I found more troubling political agendas aiming to change the current political map of the region, which would not only drag the region into another wave of serious conflicts, especially sectarianism, but also expose the region to higher level of dependency on the West through new alliances. It is my assumption that these new alliances would focus on political issues so as to create superficial stability but not to address educational, economic, or social challenges that now face the region. While the US government denies the allegations of a new Middle East map, we observe today many *serious* indications of recent movement in the region, such as the Arab Spring, Syria's condition, Iraq, the new American-Iranian relationship, and the current US-Russian conflicting agenda in the region. These developments sadly do not promise a brighter future.

If we examine the genesis of the G8–BMENA Partnership, we find that the United States used the Arab Human Development Report of 2003, as its backbone to engage in the reform effort given the high rates of illiteracy (40 percent of all, or 65 million people), and an unemployment rate of 25 percent. However, the United Nations Human Development Report of 2015 shows that the unemployment rate in the Arab states is the highest in the world, at 29 percent, which is higher than the 2003 level. Further, it shows a minimal increase in internet usage, from 1.6 percent in 2003 to 4 percent in 2015, compared with 81 percent in developed countries. Those statistics speak to the dysfunctional types of partnerships analyzed in this research.

Methodological Implications and Further Research

This study is limited in that I used official documents produced by government officials and by representatives of civil societies and regarded them as official discourse and public discourse, respectively. As a matter of fact, this arrangement made sense for my analysis, but analyzing these documents from thirty-five countries while considering these documents as representative of all countries, under the impression that these countries had equal opportunity in influencing the drafting process of the documents, may have given me only a general understanding of this type of partnership. And at the same time, it did not reveal the smallest details in the discourse and the level of participation of each country. In other words, we already know that the official entity had control over the discourse of the partnership, but I am not certain if the official discourse was overly controlled by the G8, by the BMENA representatives, or by a specific country, and the research did not reveal if the BMENA countries were involved in the partnership only for public appeal and not for real reform.

On the other hand, considering civil societies as true representatives of the public discourse may have swayed my analysis, because those representatives—even though they do not work in or represent the governments in this partnership—may not necessarily represent the people's discourse. That is to say, there were no elections to choose the representatives; instead, they were chosen by their respective countries. Take for example this statement from the 2012 annual G8–BMENA meeting:

> At the Forum for the Future in Tunisia, we had strong ministerial and other high-level participation from BMENA and G-8 countries, as well as representatives from international organizations and international financial institutions. *Forty-five civil society and private sector leaders were selected from over 125 participants* [emphasis added] to present their platforms and dialogue with ministers. (p. 5)

In other words, I could not ascertain the criteria by which civil societies were chosen from the rest of the 125 participants. This was not clarified in any of the analyzed documents, even though some of the civil societies do not claim that they represent the public. Therefore, it is my claim that they brought a different angle to my research in identifying discourse control and hegemonic relations not only between the G8 and BMENA countries but also between the partnership and civil societies and the public as a whole. This means I was not able in this research to exhaust all public discourse, but the public discourse that I did examine was a representation of an entity other than the dominant one. It is also important to consider that unequal political and economic powers exist between countries in the region, and this might have affected their representation in the annual meetings on both the official and public levels. For example, Afghanistan may not have the same level of representation as Saudi Arabia or Egypt.

Furthermore, I limited my study to critically analyze documents produced by an international entity to examine power relations between the G8 and BMENA countries as an example of power relations between the West and the East. Even though my methodology gave me the ability to uncover important information and a global structure that reinforces its control over the region in a different and some may call a dangerous manner. I do not believe it was entirely ethical or moral manner considering what is at stake not only for the region but also for the world. While I argued that hegemonic influence was found in both types of discourses on different levels, this does not prove my theory with certainty or eliminate the existence of hegemonic influence from the larger official discourse or the *people's* discourse. Put simply, first, adding another layer of macro-level analysis by including a higher level of government representation, and second, including people's discourse (not the public discourse by civil societies), could have resulted in a more accurate representation of both official discourse and the people's discourse.

Therefore, it may have been more appropriate to employ a critical ethnographic approach to investigate the concept of hegemony in the region from three angles—the official, the public, and the people's—to give me a macro-level understanding of the situation. It is almost impossible to engage in such research with all of the twenty-seven BMENA countries that participated in the partnership, but taking one country that may have all or most commonality with the rest of the region might be a goal of future research. While ethnography contributes to the sum of knowledge, it came under great criticism because it was considered an academic exercise (Atkinson & Hammersley, 1994) with little constructive value. This is the reason for suggest the utilization of critical ethnography, which could have been a better approach for this type of research. Madison (2005) depicts critical ethnography as the following:

> Critical ethnography begins with an ethical responsibility to address processes of unfairness or injustice within a particular *lived* domain. By "ethical responsibility" I mean a compelling sense of duty and commitment based on moral principles of human freedom and well-being, and hence a compassion for the suffering of living being. The conditions for existence within a particular context are not as they could be for specific subjects; as a result, the researcher feels a moral obligation to make a contribution towards changing those conditions toward greater freedom and equity ... the critical ethnographer resists domestication and moves from "what is" to "what could be." (p. 5)

This means disturbing the status quo by exposing power and control dynamics in marginalized communities. It means identifying my privileges, my skills, and my resources as a researcher to counter the dominant discourse and to bring the marginalized voices forward. Furthermore, critical ethnography contributes to the local and global knowledge of emancipation and it supports a discourse of social justice. If we do not do that, then the alternative would be a continuous dialogue stemming from uncritical thinking characterized by conformity, which at the end of day prevents subordinate communities and countries from imagining new possibilities. It is an approach that not only focuses on the use and abuse of power but also calls for action and practice. This is why Barbour (2007) calls for leadership training for ethnographers, not just to critically understand power relations but also to create clubs and partnerships for actions for the concerned people in marginalized communities and for critical researchers worldwide.

Closing Remarks

According to my analysis, the G8–BMENA Partnership did not have a good foundation from the inception, mainly because it was drafted and designed by the United States and did not generate the support needed to be fruitful, even on a superficial level. It was military power that preceded its foundation, namely the invasion of Iraq in 2003, that created negative sentiments for some of the BMENA governments, some of the civil societies, and the public, which fact prevented some reforms from materializing. The US-led partnership used political power (soft power) to create a superficial collaboration with the G8 countries and convince them to work with the United States in its effort to shape educational, economic, and social "reforms" in the region by simply focusing on the labor market demands. This has provided the region with small projects concerned with illiteracy rates, unemployment issues, and security, and has opened the region's markets further to the United States and Europe. As stated, these issues rank as a second-level concern, because real reform should have originated from the region and with a genuine interest by the G8 to march toward successful reforms.

In my assessment, the partnership had obvious control over the region's educational, societal, economic, and political spheres, which is not a new phenomenon. A hundred years ago, a more coercive agreement was struck between two major powers at the time (Britain and France): the infamous Sykes–Picot Agreement of 1916, which drew the border map for the entire Middle East region. To make matters worse, at least on self-esteem and psychological levels, Sykes–Picot even designed the flags of many countries (Aljazeera, 2014). The G8–BMENA Partnership may have taken a softer approach in changing the region, but the future does not look promising, especially after the "Blood Borders" map surfaced in the *American Armed Forces Journal* (2006) along with an article written by Ralph Peters, who is considered the American Sykes–Picot for the region. The new Middle East might be an ongoing project led by the United States covertly, and perhaps the Arab Spring facilitated that endeavor, and yet again we see the "Blood Borders" map suggesting that the Sykes–Picot Agreement was a deformed effort serving the European interests in 1916 and that the new borders will help correct that deformity (The Huffington Post, 2015). In other words, it is good for the region, and the region is passively waiting for the change.

My analysis showed that the G8–BMENA Partnership used soft discourse to numb people's emotions, either those in civil society organizations or the general public, so as to achieve its hidden purposes. It used international organizations such as the World Bank to highlight the miserable conditions in the BMENA educationally, socially, and economically (United Nations Development Program, 2002). It also highlighted the security concerns and the threat of terrorism if no action was taken by the local governments, and the possible ramifications, such as overthrowing its leaders. It pinned the local governments into a corner, forcing them to join the partnership and be part of it to publicly save face, saying that in return there would be some benefits for the region. Keep in mind that BMENA governments need political, military, and economic support either to keep the status quo or at least to prevent conditions from worsening. Here, we observe the concept of smart power (Girdner, 2004) that combines both "hard power, military action" and "soft power, political" influence to maintain the hegemonic relationship.

According to van Dijk (2001b) and his understanding of group power, it was observed in the partnership that the G8–BMENA discourse was controlled by the official group consisting of the G8 and BMENA countries. First, controlling the discourse is a symbolic power that is reflected in the number of documents produced by the G8–BMENA Partnership, which was thirty-two (78 percent) of the forty-one of documents. This showcases the clear domination by governments over the discourse.

The nature of the discourse observed in the partnership is what van Dijk (1996) describes as passive discourse, like the type we see in interactions between ordinary people and with police or with judges, because it shows that neither BMENA representatives nor civil society representatives had control over the interaction, being passively on the receiving end. Furthermore, the G8 had more access to discourse and therefore was able not only to control the discourse but also to control the properties and influence the partnership dynamics. However, van Dijk (2001b) cautions us against considering only text control as the embodiment of power relations in a group interaction, saying that rather it is the context control that matters, because this is what reinforces the dynamics of a relationship. *Context* here means "the mentally represented structure of those properties of the social situation that are relevant for the production or comprehension of discourse" (van Dijk 2001b, p. 356).

van Dijk (2001b) explains the concept of discourse control and its relation to mind control very eloquently, stating that the first step of control is to control the dominant discourse, which was the case in this study. The second step is through mind control, which in essence reproduces dominance in a given society. Consequently, the BMENA governments and civil society organizations, with their lower status, come to acquire their beliefs, opinions, and knowledge from powerful organizations such as the G8, for different reasons. First, G8 discourse was considered legitimate and trustworthy because it was produced by advanced nations in all areas of the proposed reform, such as education and economy. Second, because the partnership was created by the United States, the BMENA governments then were required to be part of the annual meetings and to come with joint declarations at least to save face and show their populations that they were working to improve people's lives. Third, civil society organizations contributed to the general discourse, but they are at the lowest level of power, and when their discourse deviated dramatically from the general guidelines established by the partnership, they were blocked or othered. This was observed in many instances throughout the analysis; nonetheless, the civil societies were able to produce slightly more long-lasting positive recommendations. In other words, the dominant group had the ability to limit an alternative discourse or at least to marginalize it. Fourth, the G8–BMENA dynamic was interesting, to say the least, because the governments met together in a closed fashion, and the civil societies conducted parallel meetings, which is a clear observation of exclusion. Following are two comments that speak to the group power in light of exclusion and othering:

> Unfortunately, the Arab world, except for Morocco, did not witness such frameworks and mechanisms allowing direct interaction between the government and the representatives of the civil society. Most of the Arab states reject dialogue on equal footing with the civil society actors unless in an international or regional non-Arab forums! [emphasis added] (2012 G8–BMENA Initiative, 2004, p. 2)

> Consequently, serious inquiries arise among the circles of the civil society regarding the added value of the direct participation in the proceedings of the Forum for the Future. Why not then restricting

> such participation to mailing the recommendations
> of the civil society [emphasis added] for saving ef-
> forts and money and avoiding delusion of the public
> opinion that the civil society is a real partner in the
> Forum. (2012 G8-BMENA Initiative, 2004, p. 11)

As far as the social consequences of domination go, I can draw
from personal experience and recent interaction when I was a guest
speaker (A. Abumilha, personal communication, September 1,
2016) with twelve international students from six countries (Brazil,
China, Japan, Saudi Arabia, South Korea, and Taiwan) to whom
I introduced my research. All are in the United States to pursue
their educational dream, and it seems that they have given up on
their countries. They see Western education as the best option
for professional, social, and economic success. They needed more
English-language teaching because they want to advance along
the professional and socioeconomic ladder. They needed Western
degrees and qualifications because they believed these would provide them with social and cultural capital or what Bourdieu (1977)
calls "habitus." They thought that reform comes only by adapting
to the Western model beyond education. It was astonishing to me
when I told them that I hoped in my lifetime that our countries
would limit sending students to the United States or Europe, saying
that each country can build its own capacity in medicine, science,
engineering, and technology, and that the next generation can produce knowledge from their respective homelands using their native
languages. The reaction of these twelve international students was
hard to describe, but I can claim that they were shocked because
they considered my vision neither feasible nor realistic. That is the
social consequence that I am afraid of seeing happen when marginalized people lose even the hope to change the status quo. It is

the mental colonization that scares me the most, and that, I believe, is the ultimate barrier to reform in the BMENA region and in all marginalized nations.

Limitations

The major limitation in this research was the unavailability of identical documents for each year of the needed analysis from 2004 to 2013. For example, the G8–BMENA Partnership did not produce a joint declaration or a chair's summary for its annual meetings every year. Even though I contacted governmental organizations and civil societies in the United States, Canada, Germany, Oman, Tunisia, and Egypt, those correspondences were not fruitful in either gaining access to the needed documents or at least understanding the reasoning for their unavailability to the public. I was able to find documents for each year from 2004 to 2013, but they were not on the same level of details. Another obstacle I faced was the fact that I was not able to collect any documents after 2013 or any reliable information, and therefore I was not able to establish any general conclusions about the fate of the G8–BMENA Partnership. It seems that the partnership dissolved without any announcement to researchers or its followers.

REFERENCES

(NAFSA) National Association of Foreign Student Advisers. (2012). *The Economic Benefits of International Students to the U.S. Economy Academic Year 2011-2012.* Bloomington: Institute of International Education's Open Doors.

(NAFSA) National Association of Foreign Student Advisers. (2013, 11, 5). *Scholarships Bring Record Number of Saudi Students to United States.* Retrieved from Explore international education: http://www.nafsa.org/Explore_International_Education/In_the_News/Scholarships_Bring_Record_Number_of_Saudi_Students_to_United_States/

2012 G8-BMENA Initiative. (2008, 10, 19). *9th Forum for the Future.* Retrieved from 2012 G8-BMENA Initiative: http://www.forumforfuture.org/english/eDocuments.aspx

2012 G8-BMENA Initiative. (2009, 11, 2). *9th Forum for the Future.* Retrieved from 2012 G8-BMENA Initiative: http://www.forumforfuture.org/english/eDocuments.aspx

2012 G8-BMENA Initiative. (2011, 11, 21). *9th Forum for the Future.* Retrieved from 2012 G8-BMENA Initiative: http://www.forumforfuture.org/english/eDocuments.aspx

2012 G8-BMENA Initiative. (2012). *9ʰ Forum for the Future*. Retrieved from 2012 G8-BMENA Initiative: http://www.forumforfuture.org/english/eDocuments.aspx

2012 G8-BMENA Initiative. (2004, 12). *9ʰ Forum for the Future*. Retrieved from 2012 G8-BMENA Initiative: http://www.forumforfuture.org/english/eDocuments.aspx

2012 G8-BMENA Initiative. (2005, 11, 12). *9ʰ Forum for the Future*. Retrieved from 2012 G8-BMENA Initiative: http://www.forumforfuture.org/english/eDocuments.aspx

2012 G8-BMENA Initiative. (2010, 11, 7). *9ʰ Forum for the Future*. Retrieved from 2012 G8-BMENA Initiative: http://www.forumforfuture.org/english/eDocuments.aspx

Abir, M. (1988). *Saudi Arabia in the oil Era regime and elites; conflict and collaboration*. London: Croom Helm Ltd.

Abo-Arrad, S. (2004). The Educational System in the Kingdom of Saudi Arabia and Challenges of Globalization. *King Saud University*, 1-28.

Akkari, A. (2004). Education in the Middle East and North Africa: The Current Situation and Future Challenges. *International Education*, 144-153.

Al Hayat Arabic Newspaper. (2004, 2, 13). *President Bush's "Greater Middle East Partnership Initiative"*. Retrieved from Al Hayat Arabic Newspaper: https://www.hks.harvard.edu/fs/pnorris/Acrobat/AlHayat%20Article.pdf

Al-Abed Al Haq, F., & Smadi, O. (1996). Spread of English and westernization in Saudi Arabia. *World Englishes*, 307-317.

Alexander, K. (1994). The Purpose of Education: Peace, Capitalism and Nationalism. *Journal of Education Finance*, 17-28.

Al-Hazmi, S. (2003). EFL teacher preparation programs in Saudi Arabia: Trends and challenges. *TESOL Quarterly*, 341-344.

Al-Hazmi, S. (2006). English and Arabization: Friends or foes?": The Saudi experience. *Proceedings of the 8ᵗʰ English in Southeast Asia Conference*. Kuala Lumpur: University of Malay.

Al-Jarf, R. S. (2004a). College students' attitudes towards using English and Arabic as a medium of instruction. *Globalization and E'ducation Priorities* (pp. 1-15). Riyadh, Saudi Arabia: King Saud University.

Al-Jarf, R. S. (2004b). Should We Teach English to Children Under the Age of Six? *Early Childhood: Its characteristics and needs* (pp. 1-28). Riyadh, Saudi Arabia: King Saud University.

Al-Jarf, R. S. (2005). The role of higher education institutions in the Arabization process. *Languages in the Era of Globalization* (pp. 1-18). Riyadh: King Saud University.

Aljazeera (Director). (2014). *World War One Through Arab Eyes* [Motion Picture]. Retrieved from https://www.aljazeera.com/programmes/specialseries/2014/11/world-war-one-through-arab-eyes-20141114133936678600.html

Allam, A. (2011, April 25). *Saudi Education Reforms Face Resistance*. Retrieved Dec 10, 2012, from Financial Times: http://

www.ft.com/intl/cms/s/0/07607fb0-6f5d-11e0-952c-00144feabdc0.html#axzz2EhBvbJx5

Allen, R. L. (2001). The globalization of the white supermacy: Toward a critical discourse on the racialization of the world. *Educational Theory*, 467-485.

Altbach, P. (2006). *International higher education: Reflections on policy and practice.* Chestnut Hill: Center for International Higher Education, Boston College.

Al-Zoman, A. H. (2003). *Supporting the Arabic language in domain names.* Riyadh, Saudi Arabia.

Appadurai, A. (1996). *Modernity at large: Cultural dimensions of globalization.* Minneapolis, MN: University of Minnesota Press.

Apple, M. W. (1979). *Ideology and curriculum.* London: Routledge and Kegan Paul.

Apple, M. (1990). *On analyzing hegemony. In M. Apple, Ideology and curriculum (2nd.) (pp.1-25).* New York: Routledge.

Armed Forces Journal. (2006, June). *Peters' "Blood borders" map.* Retrieved from Armed Forces Journal: http://armedforces-journal.com/peters-blood-borders-map/

Aronowitz, S. (1988). *Science as power: Discourse and ideology in modern society.* Minneapolis: The University of Minnesota Press.

Atkinson, P., & Hammersley, M. (1994). Ethnography and participant observation. In N. Denzin, & Y. Lincoln, *Handbook of qualitative research* (pp. 485-499). Thousand Oaks, CA: Sage.

Babrakzai, F. (2002). Response to Salah Troudi's article,"English as a language of instruction in the UAE: What is the hidden message? Perspectives: An English Language Teaching Periodical. *TESOL Arabia*, 42-46.

Baker, V. (1997). Does does formalism spell failure? Values and pedagogies in cross-cultural perspective. In G. Spindler, *Education and cultural process: anthropological approaches* (pp. 454-471). Long Grove, IL: Waveland Press.

Barber, B. (1996). *Jihad vs. McWorld*. New York: Ballantine.

Barbour. (2007). Leader paradoxes and critical ethnographies. *Academic Exchange Quarterly*, 117-121.

Bourdieu, P. (1977). *Outline of a theory of practice*. Cambridge, UK: Cambridge University Press.

Bourdieu, P. (1984). *Home Academicus*. Paris: Minuit.

Bourdieu, P., Passeron, J. C., & Saint-Martin, M. (1994). *Academic discourse linguistic misunderstanding and professorial power.* Cambridge: Polity Press.

Bradac, J. J., Hemphill, M. R., & Tardy, C. H. (1981). Language style on trial: effects of "powerful" and "powerless"speech upon judgments of victims and villains. *Western Journal of Speech Communication*, 327-341.

Brecher, J., Costello, T., & Smith, B. (2002). *Globalization from below: The power of solidarity*. Cambridge, MA: South End Press.

Bremmer, I. (2004). The Saudi paradox. *World Policy Journal*, 23-30.

Brichs, F. I. (2013). *Political Regimes in the Arab World: Society and the Exercise of Power.* New York: Routledge.

Broader Middle East & North Africa Initiative. (2005, 7, 1). Retrieved from G8 Research Group: http://www.g8.utoronto.ca/evaluations/2004seaisland_final/01_2004_seaisland_final.pdf

Broader Middle East and North Africa initiative. (2004, 11, 25). *Final Communiqui of the ABC Annual Conference.* Retrieved from U.S. State Department: https://2005-2009-bmena.state.gov/rls/55654.htm

Broadfoot, P. (2001). *An introduction to assessment.* London: Viva-Continuum.

Bryan, L., & Farrell, D. (1996). *Market unbound: Unleashing global capitalism.* New York: John Wiley & Sons.

Cameron, D. (2002). *Globalization and the teaching of communication skills. In D. Block & D. Cameron (Eds.), Globalization and language teaching (pp. 67-82).* London: Routledge.

Canagarajah, A. S. (1999). *Resisting linguistic imperialism in English teaching.* Oxford: Oxford University Press.

Canagarajah, A. S. (2005). Accommodating tensions in language-in-education policies: An afterword. In A. M. Lin, & P. W. Martin, *Decolonisation, globalisation language-in-education policy and practice (Ed.),* (pp. 194-201). Clevedon: Multilingual Matters LTD.

Chatham House. (2013, 12, 8). *Middle East and North Africa Summary.* Retrieved from Chatham House: https://www.chathamhouse.

org/sites/files/chathamhouse/home/chatham/public_html/sites/default/files/Dec13BMENAWorkshop.pdf

Clary, C., & Karlin, M. (2011). Saudi Arabia's Reform Gamble. *Survival Global Politics and Strategy,* 15-20.

Conrad, A. W. (1996). *The international role of English: The state of the discussion. In J. A. Fishman, A. W. Conrad & A. Rubal-Lopez (Ed.), Post-imperial English: Status change in former British and American colonies, 1940-1990 (pp. 13-36).* Berlin: Mouton de Gruyter.

Conway, D. (1995). *Classical liberalism: The unvanquished ideal.* London: Macmillan.

Crystal, D. (2002). *English as a global language.* Cambridge, UK: Cambridge University Press.

Cunningham, F. (1987). False consciousness. In *Democratic theory and socialism* (pp. 236—267). Cambridge: Cambridge University Pres.

Dale, R. (1999). Specifying globalization effects on national policy: a focus on the mechanisms. *Journal Of Education Policy, 4,* 1-7.

Danet, B. (1984). Legal Discourse. *Text - An Interdisciplinary Journal for the Study of Discourse*(4 Special Issue), 1-8.

Denman, B. D., & Hilal, K. T. (2011). From barriers to bridges: An investigation on Saudi student mobility (2006-2009). *International Review of Education,* 299-318.

Donn, G., & Al Mathri, Y. (2010). *Globalisation and Higher Education in the Arab GUlf States*. Oxford: Symposium Books Ltd.

Economist Global Agenda. (2002, 01 2010). *The world's educator*. Retrieved from The Economist: http://www.economist.com/node/1141777

Eltantawy, N., & Wiest, J. B. (2011). Social Media in the Egyptian revolution: Reconsidering resource mobilization theory. *International Journal of Communication*, 1207–1224.

Elyas, T. (2008). The attitude and the impact of the American English as a global language within the Saudi education system. *Novitsa-Royal*, 28-48.

Erhan, C. (2005). Broader Middle East and North Africa Initiative and Beyond. *Journal of International Affairs*, 153-170.

Eurostat. (2001). *Information society statistics..* Luxembourg: Office for Official Publications of the European Communities.

Fairclough, N. (1989). *Language and power*. London: Longman.

Fairclough, N. (1992). *Discourse and social change*. Cambridge: Polity Press.

Fairclough, N. (1995). *Critical discourse analysis: The critical study of language*. London: Longman.

Fairclough, N., & Wodak, R. (1997). Critical discourse analysis. In T. A. van Dijk, *Discourse as interaction* (pp. 258-284). London: Sage.

Farhat, E. (2011, 1, 31). *Qatar forum, will it be the last?* في «المستقبل منتدى الدوحة.. هل يكون الأخير؟*. Retrieved from Alanba Newspaper: http://www.alanba.com.kw/weekly/arabic-international-news/reports-and-issues/168715/31-01-2011

Featherstone, M. (1996). *Localism, globalization, and cultural identity. In R. Wilson & W. Dissanayake (Eds.), Global/local: Cultural production and the transnational imaginary (pp.46-77)*. Durham, NC: Duke University Press.

Federal Ministry of Education and Research. (2006, 6, 1). *Documents*. Retrieved from The Sultanate of Oman Ministry of Education: http://www.g8-bmena-education.de/_media/ Moscow_Declaration_June_2006.pdf

Federal Ministry of Education and Research. (2006). *Documents*. Retrieved from The Sultanate of Oman Ministry of Education: http://www.g8-bmena-education.de/en/162.php

Federal Ministry of Education and Research. (2006-2007, May). *Follow-up to the G8-BMENA Educational Ministerial, Sharm El Sheikh*. Retrieved from The Sultanate of Oman Ministry of Education: https://view.officeapps.live.com/op/view. aspx?src=http://www.g8-bmena-education.de/_me-dia/13_Progress_since_Sharm_el_Sheikh.doc

Federal Ministry of Education and Research. (2007, 11, 20). *Documents*. Retrieved from The Sultanate of Oman Ministry of Education: http://www.g8-bmena-education.de/_media/ Tertiary_Education_new_working_group.pdf

Federal Ministry of Education and Research. (2007, 11, 21). *Documents*. Retrieved from The Sultanate of Oman Ministry of Education: http://www.g8-bmena-education.de/_media/ Cross-cutting_issues_paper_including_statistical_annex.pdf

Federal Ministry of Education and Research. (2007, 11, 20). *Documents*. Retrieved from The Sultanate of Oman Ministry of Education: http://www.g8-bmena-education.de/_media/ Outcomes_Senior_Officials_Meeting.ENG.pdf

Federal Ministry of Education and Research. (2007, 11, 21). *Documents*. Retrieved from Federal Ministry of Education and Research: http://www.g8-bmena-education.de/

Federal Ministry of Education and Research. (n.d.). *Documents*. Retrieved from The Sultanate of Oman Ministry of Education: http://www.g8-bmena-education.de/_media/ co_chairs_English_final.pdf

Federal Ministry of Education and Research. (2006, 5, 23). *Documents*. Retrieved from The Sultanate of Oman Ministry of Education: http://www.g8-bmena-education.de/_media/ G8-BMENA-declaration-2006-05-en.pdf

Federal Ministry of Education and Research Oman. (2005, 5, 23). *Documents*. Retrieved from The Sultanate of Oman Ministry of Education: http://www.g8-bmena-education.de/_media/ Dead_Sea_Ministerial_on_Education__Jordan_05.pdf

Fishman, J. A. (2006). *Language policy and language shift. In T. Ricento (Ed.), An introduction to language policy (pp. 311-328)*. Malden, MA: Blackwell.

Fitzsimons, P. (2000). Changing conceptions of globalization: Changing conceptions of education. *Educational Theory*, 347-367.

Forum for the Future. (2004, 12, 11). Retrieved from Forum for the Future: www.g8.utoronto.ca/meetings-official/forumforfuture_041211.pdf.

Fowler, R. (1985). *Handbook of discourse analysis.* London: Academic Press.

Giddens, A. (1991). *Modernity and self-identity.* Stanford, CA: Stanford University Press.

Girdner, E. J. (2004). Pre-emptive war: The case of Iraq. *Journal of International Affairs*, 5-30.

Giroux, H. (1981). *Ideology, culture, and the process of schooling.* London: Falmer Press.

Gow, H. B. (1989). The True Purpose of Education. *The Phi Delta Kappan*, 545-546.

Gramsci, A. (1971). *Prison notebooks.* New York: International Publishers.

Gramsci, A. (2000). *Some aspects of the souther question. In D. Forgace (Ed.), The Antonio Gramsci reader: Selected writings 1916-1935 (pp. 171-185).* New York: New York University Press.

Gray, J. (2002). *The global coursebook in English language teaching. In D. Block & D. Carmeron (Eds.), Globalization and language teaching (pp. 151-167).* London: Routledge.

Hall, S. (1997). *The local and the global:Globalization and ethnicity. In A. D. King (Ed.), Culture, globalization and the world system: Contemporary conditions for the representation of identity (pp.19-39).* Minneapolis, MN: University of Minnesota Press.

Halliday, M. A. (1994). *Introduction to functional grammar.* London: Arnold.

Harvey, D. (1990). *The condition of postmodernity.* Cambridge, MA: Blackwell.

Herder, J. G. (1772-2002). *Treaties on the origin of language. In M. N. Forster (Ed.), Herder: Philsophical writings (pp. 65-164).* Cambrige, UK: Cambrige University Press.

Hirst, P., & Thompson, G. (1995). Globalization and the future of the nation-state. *Economy and Society,* 408-442.

Hodge, R., & Kress, G. R. (1993). *Language as ideology.* London: Routledge.

Hoey, M. (1996). A clause-relational analysis of selected dictionary entries: Contrast and compatibility in the definitions of 'man' and 'woman.'. In C. R. Caldas-Coulthard, & M. Coulthard, *Texts and practices: Readings in critical discourse analysis* (pp. 150-165). London: Sage.

Hoogvelt, A. (2001). *Globalization and the postcolonial world: The New Political Economy of Development.* Baltimore: Johns Hopkins University Press.

Humboldt, W. (1836/1988). *On language: The diversity of human language-structureand its influence on the mental development of mankind.* Cambridge, UK: Cambridge University Press.

Jameson, F. (1998). *Notes on globalization as philosophical issue. In F. Jameson & M. Miyoshi (Eds), The culture of globalization (pp. 54-77).* Durham, NC: Duke University Press.

Jordon, A. T. (2011). *The Makiing of the Modern Kingdom Globalization and Chnage in Saudi Arabia.* Long Grove, IL: Waveland Press, INC.

Kachru, B. B. (1984). *The alchemy of English: Social and functional power of non-native varieties. In M. Schulz & W. M. O'Barr (Eds.), Language and power (pp. 176-193).* THousand Oaks, CA: Sage.

Kachru, B. B., & Nelson, C. L. (2001). *World Englishes. In A. Burns & C. Coffin (Eds.), Analysing English in a global context, (pp. 9-25).* London: Routledge.

Kaldor, M. (1981). *The baroque arsenal.* New York: Farrar, Straus & Giroux.

Kaplan, R. B. (2001). *English-the accidental language of science. In U. Ammon(Ed.), the dominace of English as a language of science (pp. 3-26).* Berlin:: Mouton de Gruyter.

Kawai, Y. (2004). Globalization, the global spread of the English language, and the nation: a critical narrative analysis of Japanese nationalism and identities in a globalization context (Doctoral dissertation). *Retrieved from UNM LIBROS Catalog,* unm.b3966326.

Khashan, H. (1984). A Study of Student Perceptions in a Saudi Arabian University. *Research in Higher Education*, 17-31.

King, F. (1995). *Neo-Liberalism: Theoretical problems and practical inconsistencies. In M, Mills & F. King (Eds.), The promise of liberalism: A comparative analysis of consensus politics.* Aldershot, U.K.: Dartmouth.

Kurtz, S. (2012, Aug, 31). *Thanks to Scholarship, Saudi Students Return to U.S. in Droves.* Retrieved Dec 11, 2012, from The Washington Diplomat: http://www.washdiplomat.com/index.php?option=com_content&view=article&id=8544:thanks-to-scholarship-saudi-students-return-to-us-in-droves&catid=1492:september-2012&Itemid=501

Kvale, S. (1996). *Interviews: An introduction to qualitative research interviewing.* Thousand Oaks: Sage.

Lawn, M. (2006). Soft governance and the learning spaces of Europe. *Comparative European Politics*, 272-288.

Lingard, R. L. (2000). It is and it isn't: Vernacular globalization, educational policy, and restructuring. In N. C. Burbules, & C. A. Torres, *Globalization and Education: Critical Perspectives* (pp. 79-108). London: Routledge.

Luciani, G. (1990). *The Arab state.* London: Routledge.

Macedo, D., Dendrinos, B., & Gounari, P. (2003). *The hegemony of English.* Boulder, CO: Paradigm Publishers.

Madison, S. (2005). *Critical ethnography methods, ethics, and performance.* Thousand Oaks: Sage Publications.

Maroun, N., Samman, H., Moujaes, C., & Abouchakra, R. (2008). How to Succeed at Education Reform: The Case for Saudi Arabia and Broader GCC Region. *Ideation Center Insights*, 1-25.

Martin, J. N., & Nakayama, T. K. (2007). *Intercultural communication in context*. New York: The McGraw-Hill Companies, Inc.

Martin, P. (2000). *The moral case for globalization. In F. J. Lechner & J. Boli (Eds.), The globalization reader*. Malden, MA: Blackwell.

Marx, K., & Engels, F. (1848/1985). *The Communist manifesto*. London: Penguin.

Mauranen, A. (2003). The corpus of English as lingua franca in academic settings. *TESOL Quarterly*, 513-527.

Middle East and North Africa Democracy Program. (2006, 6, 25). Retrieved from No Peace without Justice: http://www. npwj.org/MENA/International-Conference-Democracy-Political-Reforms-and-Freedom-Expression.html-0

Mill, J. S. (1861/2001). *Considerations on representative government. In V. P. Pecora (Ed.), Nations and identities: Classic readings, (pp. 142-148)*. Malden, MA: Blackwell.

Ministry of Higher Education (MOHE). (2013, 11, 08). *Ministry of Higher Education Budget 2013*. Retrieved from A glance on the budget: http://www.mohe.gov.sa/ar/Pages/Budget.aspx

Miyoshi, M. (1993). A bordless world? From colonialism to transnationlism and the decline of the nation-state. *Cultural Inquriy*, 726-751.

Moaddel, M. (2006). The Saudi Public Speaks: Religion, Gender, and Politics. *International Journal of Middle East Studies*, 79-108.

National Human Rights Committee. (2011, 1, 14). *Forum Concludes; No Joint Declaration*. Retrieved from National Human Rights Committee: http://www.nhrc-qa.org/en/forum-concludes-no-joint-declaration/

Nazemroaya, M. D. (2006, November). *Plans for Redrawing the Middle East: The Project for a "New Middle East"*. Retrieved from Center for Research and Globalization: http://www.globalresearch.ca/plans-for-redrawing-the-middle-east-the-project-for-a-new-middle-east/3882

Neal, M., & Finlay, J. L. (2007). American Hegemony and Business Education in the Arab World. *Journal of Management Education*, 38-82.

Ng, S. H., & Bradac, J. J. (1993). *Power in language.* Newbury Park: Sage.

Nieuwenhuijze, V. (1965). *Social Stratification and the Middle East.* Leiden, Netherlands: E. J. Brill.

Noi, A. U. (2011). *The Euro-Mediterranean Partnership and the Broader Middle East and North Africa Initiative.* Lanham: University Press of America.

O'Barr, W. M., Conley, J. M., & Lind, A. (1978). The power of language: presentational style in the courtroom. *Duke Law Journal*, 1375-1399. Retrieved from http://scholarship.law.duke.edu/cgi/viewcontent.cgi?article=2686&context=dlj

Office of Her Majesty, Press Department - Dead Sea. (2005, 5, 24). *Arab-G8 Ministerial Meeting on Education*. Retrieved from Media Center: http://www.queenrania.jo/en/media/articles/arab-g8-ministerial-meeting-education

Office of the Spokesman. (2004, 12, 11). *Accomplishments of the First Forum For Future, Rabat 2004*. Retrieved from U.S. State Department: http://2001-2009.state.gov/r/pa/prs/ps/2004/39676.htm

Olaniran, B. A., & Agnello, M. F. (2008). Globalization, educational hegemony, and higher Education. *Multicultural Education and Technology*, 68-86.

Palmer, P. J. (2007). *The courage to teach: Exploring the inner landscape of a teacher's life*. San Francisco, CA: John Wiley & Sons.

Pennycook, A. (1994). *Cultural politics of English as international language*. London: Longman.

Peters, R. (2006, June 1). *How a better Middle East would look*. Retrieved from Armed Forces Journal: http://armedforces-journal.com/blood-borders/

Phillipson, R. (1992). *Linguistic imperialism*. Oxford, UK: Oxford University Press.

Pieterse, J. N. (1994). Globalization as hybridization. *International Sociology*, 658-680.

Prokop, M. (2003). Saudi Arabia: The Politics of Education. *International Affairs*, 77-89.

Reisigl, M., & Wodak, R. (2009). The discourse historical approach. In R. Wodak, & M. Meyer, *Methods of critical discourse analysis* (pp. 275-297). London: Sage.

Ritzer, G. (1996). *The McDonaldization of society: An investigation Into the changing character of contemporary social Life revised edition.* London: Pine Forge Press.

Ritzer, G. (2000). *The McDonalization of society: New century edition..* Thousand Oaks, CA: Pine Forge Press.

Ritzer, G. (2004). *The globalization of nothing.* Thousands Oaks, CA: Pine Forge Press.

Rizvi, F. (2004). Debating Globalization and Education after September 11. *Comparative Education,* 157-171.

Robertson, R. (1992). *Globalization: Social theory and global culture.* London: Sage.

Robertson, s., Novelli, M., Dale, R., Tikly, L., Dachi, H., & Alphonce, N. (2007). *Globalisation, education and development: Ideas, actors and dynamics.* London: Department for International Development.

Rossides, D. W. (1984). What Is the Purpose of Education? The Worthless Debate Continues. *Change,* 14-21.

Roy, D. A. (1992). Saudi Arabian Education: Development Policy. *Middle Eastern Studies,* 477-508.

Rugh, W. (1973). Emergence of a New Middle Class in Saudi Arabia. *Middle East Journal,* 7-20.

Rugh, W. (2002a). Education in Saudi Arabia: Choices and constraints. *Middle East Policy*, 40-55.

Rugh, W. (2002b). Arab Education: Tradition, Growth and Reform. *The Middle East Journal*, 396-414.

Saldana, J. (2013). *The coding manual for qualitative researchers.* London: SAGE Publications Ltd.

Saleh, M. A. (1986). Development of Higher Education in Saudi Arabia. *Higher Education*, 17-23.

Secretary Powell and Moroccan Foreign Minister Benaissa. (2004, 9, 24). *Chairmen's Summary*. Retrieved from U.S. State Department: https://2005-2009-bmena.state.gov/rls/55657.htm

Sharp, J. M. (2005, 2, 15). *CRS Report for Congress*. Retrieved from Congressional Research Service ˜ The Library of Congress: https://www.fas.org/sgp/crs/mideast/RS22053.pdf

Shiffrin, D. (1994). *Approaches to discourse.* Cambridge, MA: Blackwell.

Smith, L. E. (1983). *English as international language: No room for linguistic chauvinism. In L. E. Smith (Ed.), Readings in English as an international language (pp. 7-11)*. Oxford, UK: Pergamon Press.

Smith, N. (1997). The satanic geographies of globalization: Unseen development in the 1990s. *Public Culture*, 169-189.

Stimson, M. J. (1980). *English language and literacy.* England: English language teaching profile British Council.

Taylor, T. (2001). Locating and conducting discourse analysis research. In M. Wetherell, S. Taylor, & S. J. Yates, *Discourse as data: A guide for analysis* (pp. 5-48). London: Sage.

The Huffington Post. (2015, 7, 26). كيف خطت دوائر صناع القرار في الغرب حدود الشرق الأوسط؟. Retrieved from The Huffington Post: http://www.huffpostarabi.com/2015/07/26/----_n_7856510. html

The White House Office of the Press Secretary. (2004, 6, 9). *G-8 Plan of Support for Reform.* Retrieved from U.S. State Department: http://2001-2009.state.gov/e/eeb/rls/fs/33376.htm

The White House Office of the Press Secretary. (2004, 6, 9). *Partnership for Progress and a Common Future with the Region of the Broader Middle East and North Africa.* Retrieved from U.S. State Department: http://2001-2009.state.gov/e/eeb/ rls/fs/33375.htm

Thompson-Miller, R., & Feagin, J. R. (2008). Jim Crow and the case for reparations: Lesson from the African diaspora. In A. J. Hattery, D. G. Embrick, & E. Smith, *Globaliztion and America (Ed.),* (pp. 47-63). Lanham, MD: Rowman & Littlefield Publishers, INC.

Tomlinson, J. (1999). *Globalization and culture.* Chicago: University of Chicago Press.

Toynbee, A. (1948). *Civilization on trial.* New Yourk: Oxford University Press.

Trial, G. T., & Winder, R. B. (1950). Modern Education in Saudi Arabia. *1*(3).

Troudi, S. (2002). English as a language of instruction in the UAE: What is the hidden message? Perspectives: An English Language Teaching Periodical. *TESOL Arabia*, 5-10.

Tsuda, Y. (2008). English hegemony and English divide. *China Media Research*, 47-55.

U. S. Department of State Archives. (2001-2009, January 20). *Broader Middle East and North Africa Initiative (BMENA)*. Retrieved from U. S. Department of State Archives: http://2005-2009-bmena.state.gov/

U.S. Department of State. (2008, 4, 30). *Country Reports on Terrorism*. Retrieved from U.S. Department of State: http://www.state.gov/j/ct/rls/crt/2007/104117.htm

U.S. Department of State. (2012, 12, 14). *2012 G8-BMENA Forum for the Future*. Retrieved from U.S. Department of State: http://www.state.gov/r/pa/prs/ps/2012/12/202070.htm

U.S. Department of State. (2013, 12, 17). *U.S. Intervention Delivered at the 10th Annual G-8-BMENA Forum for the Future*. Retrieved from U.S. Department of State: http://www.state.gov/j/drl/rls/rm/2013/218858.htm

U.S. Department of State. (2004, 9, 21). بيان حقائق: مبعوثون من الدول الصناعية الثماني الكبرى ودول الشرق الأوسط الكبير يناقشون في نيويورك قضايا الإصلاح. Retrieved from U.S. Department of State IIP Digital: http://iipdigital.usembassy.gov/st/arabic/texttrans/2004/09/20040921124525aywalhsib-le0.4120709.html#axzz4IxSJzDbl

U.S. Department of State. (2006, 11, 30). *2006 Forum for the Future Chairman's Summary.* Retrieved from U.S. Department of State: https://2005-2009-bmena.state.gov/rls/fs/77432.htm

U.S. Department of State Archives. (2001-2009, January 20). *Broader Middle East and North Africa Initiative (BMENA).* Retrieved from U. S. Department of State Archives: http://2005-2009-bmena.state.gov/

UNESCO. (2005, Oct. 20). *Convention on the Protection and Promotion of the Diversity of Cultural Expressions 2005.* Retrieved from United Nations Educational, Scientific and Cultural Organization: http://portal.unesco.org/en/ev.php-URL_ID=31038&URL_DO=DO_TOPIC&URL_SECTION=201.html#STATE_PARTIES

United Nations Conference on Trade and Development. (2002). World investment report 2002: Transnational corporations and export competitiveness. New York: United Nations.

United Nations Development Program. (2003). *Arab Human Development Report.* New York: United Nations Publications. Retrieved from http://www.arab-hdr.org/publications/other/ahdr/ahdr2003e.pdf

United Nations Development Program. (2002). *The Arab Human Development Report.* New York: Regional Bureau for Arab States (RBAS).

van Dijk, T. A. (2001b). Critical discourse analysis. In D. Schiffrin, D. Tannen, & H. E. Hamlilton, *Handbook of discourse analysis* (pp. 352-371). Malden: Blackwell.

van Dijk, T. A. (2005). Contextual knowledge management in discourse Production, a CDA perspective. In R. Wodak, & P. Chilton, *A new agenda in (Critical) Discourse Analysis* (pp. 71-100). Amsterdam and Philadelphia: John Benjamins.

van Dijk, T. A. (2009). Critical discourse studies: A sociocognitive approach. In R. Wodak, & M. Meyer, *Methods of critical discourse analysis* (pp. 62-86). London: Sage.

van Dijk, T. A. (1993). Principles of critical discourse analysis. *Discourse and Society,* 249-283.

van Dijk, T. A. (1996). Discourse, power, and access. In C. R. Caldas-Coulthard, & M. Coulthard, *Text and practices: Readings in critical discourse analysis* (pp. 84-104). London: Sage.

van Dijk, T. A. (1997). Political discourse and racism: Describing others in Western parliaments. In S. H. Riggins, *The language and politics of exclusion: Others in discourse* (pp. 31-64). Thousand Oaks, CA: Sage.

van Dijk, T. A. (2001a). Multidisciplinary CDA: A plea for diversity. In R. Wodak, & M. Meyer, *Methods of critical dicourse analysis* (pp. 95-120). London: Sage.

Vaughan, V. C. (1914). The Nature and Purpose of Education. *New Series,* 685-697.

Volosinov, V. N. (1973). *Marxism and philosophy of language.* Cambrige, MA: Harvard University Press.

Wallerstein, I. (1974). The rise and future demise of the world capitalist system: Concept for comparative analysis. *Comparative
Studies in Society and History*, 387-415.

Wells, A. S., Carnochan, S., Slayton, J., Allen, R. L., & Vasudeva, A.
(1998). *Globalization and educational change. In A. Hargreaves,
A. Lieberman, M. Fullan & D. Hopkins (Eds.), International
handbook of educational change (part one) (pp.322-348)*. Norwell,
MA: Kluwer Academic Publishers.

Wexler, P., & Whitson, T. (1982). Hegemony and education.
Psychology and Social Theory, 31-42.

Williams, R. (1977). *Marxism and literature*. Oxford, UK: Oxfor
University Press.

Wodak, R. (1984). Determination of guilt: discourses in the courtroom. In C. Kramarae, M. Schulz, & W. M. O'Barr, *Language
and power* (pp. 89-100). Beverly Hills: Sage.

Wodak, R. (1996). *Disorders of discourse*. London: Longman.

Wodak, R. (2001a). What CDA is about: A summary of its history,
important concepts, and its developments. In R. Wodak,
& M. Meyer, *Methods of critical discourse analysis* (pp. 1-13).
London: Sage.

Wodak, R. (2001b). The discourse-historical approach. In R.
Wodak, & M. Meyer, *Methods of discourse analysis* (pp. 63-94).
London: Sage.

World Bank. (2003). *World Development Indicators*. Washington, DC.:
Oxford University Press.

Yamani, M. (2000). *Changed Identities: The challenges of the New Generation in Saudi Arabia.* London: The Royal Institute of International Affairs.

Zuhur, S. (2011). *Middle East in Focus Saudi Arabia.* Santa Barbara: ABC-CLIO.

www.ingramcontent.com/pod-product-compliance
Lightning Source LLC
Chambersburg PA
CBHW030436290526
45786CB00001B/311